Taking Hold

From Migrant Childhood to Columbia University

Francisco Jiménez

Author of *Reaching Out, Breaking Through,* and *The Circuit*

Houghton Mifflin Harcourt
Boston   New York

www.hmhco.com

Text was set in Goudy.

Library of Congress Cataloging-in-Publication Data
Jiménez, Francisco, 1943–, author.
Taking hold / by Francisco Jiménez.
p. cm.
Sequel to: The circuit, Reaching out, and Breaking through.
ISBN 978-0-547-63230-8
1. California—Social life and customs—Fiction. 2. Migrant
agricultural laborers—Fiction. 3. Mexican American families—Fiction.
4. Mexican Americans—Fiction. I. Title.
PS3560.I55T35 2014
813'.54—dc23
2014008746

Manufactured in the United States of America
DOC 10 9 8 7 6 5 4 3 2 1

4500532305

To my wife, Laura, and to our family

Francisco, Roberto, and Trampita in Tent City, Santa Maria, CA.

Acknowledgments

I am indebted to Roberto, my brother; Darlene, my sister-in-law; and my wife, Laura, for providing me with their personal recollections of the period I write about in this book and for giving me valuable editorial advice. A special thanks to other members of my immediate family—Francisco "Pancho," Lori, Miguel, Susie, Tomás, Nova, Carlo, Dario, Camille, Orlando, and Marcel—for their patience and support during the preparation of this book.

Thanks to the many teachers and students who have enjoyed reading my work and have written to ask that I continue writing more stories about my family.

I am grateful to my friends and colleagues who have also encouraged me to write—Atom Yee, Alma Gracía, Juan Velasco, Jill Pellettieri, Victor Vari, Elsa Li, and Lori Wood.

I am thankful to the staff at Columbia University archives for giving me access to historical materials; to the Creative Work Fund for giving me the opportunity to collaborate with the National Steinbeck Center; and to Santa Clara University for giving me the time to write and for valuing my work.

Lasting gratitude to my wonderful editor, Ann Rider, who gently prodded me to write this book and made valuable suggestions for improving it.

Contents

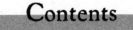

"THE JOURNEY OF OUR LIVES IS NOT JUST ABOUT THE DESTINATIONS WE HAVE REACHED. OUR WISDOM, EDUCATION AND PERSONAL GROWTH COME FROM THE PEOPLE WE MEET, THE PATHS WE CHOOSE TO FOLLOW AND THE LESSONS WE HAVE LEARNED ALONG THE WAY."

—DOLORES HUERTA

Inside the Gates

In the late afternoon of September 12, I boarded a TWA 747 in San Francisco. I was headed for graduate school at Columbia University in New York City. Although I felt grateful for having been awarded a fellowship that allowed me to continue my education at Columbia, I did not know what to expect. And leaving my family and Laura, my girlfriend, was extremely painful—I would not see them again for a very long time.

As I waited for the plane to take off, I thought about how different this journey was from the one my family and I took when we left our home in El Rancho Blanco, a small village in rural Mexico, nineteen years earlier. I was four years old at the time. We took a sluggish second-class train that had hard wooden seats from Guadalajara to Mexicali and crossed the U.S-Mexican border illegally by foot. Although we did not know where we would end up and were fearful of being caught by the *migra*, Border Patrol, my family was hopeful that we would escape our poverty and begin a new and better life.

The plane to New York finally landed at JFK Airport after a six-hour flight. It was one a.m. The opaque yellow lights in the cabin of the crowded plane went on, waking the weary passengers, who scrambled to pick up their belongings. I glanced out the narrow oval window. Blinking red lights on the tip of the wings pierced the darkness. I unbuckled my seat belt and pulled from the bin above my small brown suitcase and portable typewriter enclosed in a blue case, which my older brother, Roberto, and his wife, Darlene, had given me as a college graduation gift. All during college I had borrowed my roommates' typewriters because I could not afford my own.

I got off the plane, followed the signs to ground transportation, exited the terminal, and waited on the curb for a taxi. The stagnant air was hot, humid, and foul-smelling, like gasoline and burning rubber. A beat-up yellow cab pulled over.

"Where to?" the driver shouted through the front window. Before I had a chance to respond, he hollered again, "Come on, man, where to?"

"Columbia University," I said.

"Hop in," he yelled.

I quickly opened the back door, tossed my baggage on the seat, shut it, and opened the passenger door. "Aren't ya sitting in the back?" he asked.

"I prefer to sit in the front," I said. He rolled his eyes and grudgingly removed a pile of scattered papers and a clipboard from the passenger seat and tossed them on the dashboard. "Thank you," I said, sliding into the seat and shutting the door.

Leaning slightly forward and gripping the steering wheel with both hands, he raced out of the airport onto the freeway. I grabbed the edge of the seat and pushed both feet against the floorboard as he zigzagged past cars and trucks and went under connecting freeways that crisscrossed like concrete pretzels. We zoomed by smoke-covered industrial brick buildings with dimly lit narrow windows. On the horizon appeared clusters of grayish skyscrapers radiating startling lights. To avoid the increasingly congested traffic, the cab-driver veered off the freeway onto one-way roads that led to bumpy streets and eventually to a long, wide avenue. On both sides of it were endless massive and haggard buildings and rundown stores, entrances and display windows shielded by steel shutters that made them look like jail cells. "Are we almost there?" I asked, breaking the long silence.

He slowed down, lowered his window slightly, spit out of it, nodded, and said, "We're on Broadway and One Hundred Tenth; six more blocks." At 116th Street, he pulled over and stopped in front of a tall, wide black iron gate. "Here you are," he said. "This is the main entrance to Columbia."

"Where is Hartley Hall?" I asked. Hartley Hall was the building where I was to pick up the key to my room in John Jay Hall.

"It's at the other end of this street," he said. "Can't drive in. One hundred sixteenth is closed to traffic." We climbed out of the car. He opened the back door and reached in to get my luggage.

"I've got it, thanks." I said. He moved to the side, gave me a puzzled look, and told me the cab fare was twenty dollars. The high cost shocked me. I bit my lip, unloaded my belongings, handed him two ten-dollar bills, and thanked him.

"Good luck," he said, folding the bills in half and placing them in his shirt pocket. He got back in the car and sped off. I stood alone, glancing up at the gate. Then I picked up my typewriter case and suitcase and began walking past the gate, along a wide dark red-brick path. Suddenly an immense courtyard framed on both sides by massive buildings with Greek columns exploded into view. I stood there for a moment, marveling at their colossal size, feeling as though I were entering another world.

Almost at the end of the long walkway was a large quad with an L-shaped annex of buildings. I went down a few steps that led to a smaller quad, where a statue of Alexander Hamilton sat facing Hamilton Hall. Adjacent to Hamilton Hall was Hartley Hall. When I stepped inside, the air-conditioned lobby felt unexpectedly cool, like a church. The attendant was asleep, his bald head rolling against the back of a chair behind a desk. I feigned a cough, hoping to wake him up. It worked. He sat up, startled.

"What's up?" he said groggily. I introduced myself and

explained that I was checking in. I handed him a letter I had received from the housing office. He yawned, glanced at the clock, scratched his head, riffled through a pile of envelopes stacked neatly in alphabetical order by name, pulled out mine, and handed it to me. Inside it were my room key, a list of dorm rules, and a schedule for the week. He had me sign a receipt and pointed out my dorm, directly across from Hamilton Hall. I thanked him and tiredly made my way to my new home.

John Jay Hall was an old fifteen-story dorm reserved for graduate students. Inside, in a cramped space adjacent to the large lobby, was a faded green elevator. Scratched into the paint of its door was a message that read "A guy dropped dead from old age waiting for this elevator." I took it up to the eighth floor and exited into a long, narrow, dimly lit corridor that was painted light blue. Halfway down was my room. I opened the door and turned on the light. The room looked like a prison cell. The rectangular space was approximately six by twelve feet and sparsely furnished: a tall closet to the right and, to the left, a small stained white sink with a medicine cabinet and tarnished mirror above it; a twin bed, a worn dark brown wooden desk and chair to match, and a small desk lamp. Below the window, anchored on the dark gray vinyl floor, was an old cast-iron radiator that looked like an accordion. I pulled back the discolored blue curtains and slid open the window that looked onto 114th Street. A wave of stench and hot air rushed in, accompanied by the drone of traffic and horns and sirens. A grimy red-brick apartment building across the street framed the view. I poked my head out the window and looked straight up. The sky was hazy and starless. I slammed the window shut, closed the curtains, and curled up in bed, feeling sad and lonely. I finally fell asleep, fully clothed.

Next morning I woke up startled by the sound of jackhammers and heavy traffic. For a split second I had no idea where I was or what was happening. I got out of bed and looked out the window. A tall brick building was being demolished down the street. I sat on the edge of the bed and stared at the floor. Feeling tired, lonely, and dispirited, I took from my suitcase the notebook in which I had jotted down memories of my childhood. I had written them in college to give me courage and strength whenever I felt as I did at that moment.

I skimmed the story I wrote about my efforts to pick cotton when I was six years old. My parents used to park our old jalopy at the end of the cotton fields and leave me alone in the car to take care of Trampita, my little brother. I hated being left by myself with him while they and Roberto went off to work. Thinking that if I learned to pick cotton my parents would take me with them, one afternoon, while Trampita slept in the back seat of the car, I walked over to the nearest row and tried to pick cotton. It was harder than I thought. I picked the bolls one at a time and piled them on the ground. The shells' sharp prongs scratched my hands like a cat's claw and sometimes dug into the corner of my finger-nails and made them bleed. At the end of the day I was tired and disappointed because I had picked very little. To make things worse, I forgot about Trampita, and when my parents returned, they were upset with me because I had neglected him. He had fallen off the seat, cried, and soiled himself.

As I read other recollections, I began to relive my experiences of moving from farm to farm; following the crops; living in migrant tents and old garages; working in the fields alongside my parents and older brother, picking strawberries, grapes, cotton, and carrots; and, until I was fourteen, missing two and a half months of school every year to help my family make ends meet. When I finished reading, I felt the same strength and relief I experienced when I first wrote them.

I placed the notebook in my desk drawer and took from my wallet a worn holy card of the Virgen de Guadalupe that my father had given me the day my family dropped me off at college. "*Cuídate, mijo.*" Take care of yourself, son, he had told me. "*Recuerda ser respetuoso.*" Remember to be respect-ful. I felt my throat tighten as I recalled kissing his scarred and leathery hands when he handed me the card. I smoothed it between the palms of my hands, kissed it, and said a prayer, and then I tacked it to side of the desk and sighed.

A few minutes later my small used army trunk, which I had shipped from home, was delivered to my room. I unpacked it and hung in the closet the few clothes I had brought, the same ones I had worn the last two years in college. I placed the *Webster's Dictionary and Thesaurus* on the shelf above the desk, plugged in my small clock radio, and listened to a few popular songs—"I'm a Believer," "Help!" "Can't Get No Satisfaction," and others—while I checked my schedule. I was free all morning to tour the campus on my own, and I had an invitation to attend a reception for Woodrow Wilson Fellows in the John Jay lounge that afternoon.

I read the list of dorm rules for John Jay Hall. One of them caught my eye: "No women visitors allowed in the room at any time." I did not mind, because it was the same rule I had in college; however, it surprised me because it applied to graduate students at Columbia University, which was not church-affiliated like my alma mater, a Jesuit Catholic institution. I undressed, wrapped a towel around my waist, picked up a bar of soap, and walked down the hall to the shower room. The green shower had eight nozzles and two small rectangular windows high above the wall facing the street. The paint was cracked and chipped, and several floor tiles were broken. After taking a shower, I shaved at the small sink in my room, got dressed, and took the elevator down to the ground floor, where the dining facilities were located.

The spacious dining room in John Jay Hall was luxurious, fit for royalty. It had finely detailed wood paneling, a coffered ceiling, and leaded-glass windows with dark red curtains. Various food choices were offered, cafeteria style, and every item was individually priced. I was shocked at the high cost. I would have preferred a flat fee for an all-you-can-eat system, which I experienced my freshman year in college—not without consequences. At the end of that year I had gained thirty pounds! For the next three years I had received free room and board in exchange for being a prefect, a job that required enforcing strict dorm rules, among other less stressful duties. Even though the Woodrow Wilson Fellowship provided funds for tuition, room and board, and living expenses, I was certain I could not afford to have all my meals in that dining hall. I thought of different possibilities, including eating only twice a day, and came up with the idea of buying a single-burner electric hot plate and cooking in my room, but I decided not to do it, because I would be violating one of the dorm rules, which prohibited the use of electrical appliances. After a light breakfast I went to the housing office and picked up a list of local cafés, grocery stores and banks, a subway map, and a campus directory with brief descriptions of points of interest.

Using the campus map and directory, I went to the Chemical Bank on the corner of 110th Street and Broadway and opened a checking account. I deposited the thousand-dollar stipend I had received from the Woodrow Wilson Foundation to cover my board and living expenses for the first semester. Using that account, I wrote a cashier's check for one hundred dollars to my father to help pay for his expenses. He was living in Tlaquepaque, Mexico, with my Tía Chana, his older sister, who took care of him.

When I was a sophomore in college my father had suffered a nervous breakdown. He left our family, and returned to his native land a broken man. He experienced severe back problems resulting from doing stoop labor day after day from dawn to dusk for many years. He was no longer physically able to work in the fields, the only job he could get because he did not speak English and had no formal education. Consequently, he felt useless, a burden to our family. Often he stayed in bed all day and refused to shave, eat, or talk to anyone. None of us felt relaxed or happy around him, but we continued praying for him and being respectful. His leaving caused us deep sorrow but also was a relief for my mother, who had become the target of his dark moods.

When my father could no longer work, my family stopped following seasonal crops. We settled in Bonetti Ranch, a migrant camp in Santa Maria, a small agricultural town in the central coast of California. To support our family, Roberto and I got janitorial jobs, each of us working thirty-five hours a week while going to school. My brother worked for the Santa Maria Elementary School District, and I was employed by the Santa Maria Window Cleaners, cleaning commercial offices. All during high school I worked in the mornings before school, in the evenings, and on weekends, sweeping and dusting offices, cleaning windows and toilets, and washing and waxing floors.

At the bank, I wrote a second check, for two hundred dollars, to my mother, to help pay for food and rent. She had moved into a two-bedroom house in the outskirts of Santa

Maria with my four younger siblings a year after my father left and our old army barrack in Bonetti Ranch burned to the ground owing to faulty electrical wiring. She worked in the fields, and Trampita, the third oldest child in our family, worked part-time as a custodian while he attended high school. Roberto and Darlene also lent a hand whenever they could.

I mailed the checks and went to a local grocery store and bought things for my breakfasts: a white plastic cereal bowl, a loaf of white bread, a jar of crunchy peanut butter, a jar of blueberry jam, a box of corn flakes, and only a pint of milk, as I did not have a refrigerator. I went back to my dorm, stored the food in the closet, and toured the university grounds, starting in John Jay Hall.

Columbia was founded in 1754 by a royal charter of King George II of England and named King's College. The dormitory, built in 1925, was known as the Skyscraper Dorm because it was the tallest building on campus. It housed 484 rooms and, in the basement, the Lion's Den, a pub and snack bar with a wood-beamed ceiling and a huge fireplace. It was named after John Jay, the first chief justice of the United States Supreme Court, who graduated in the class of 1764.

A few yards to the right of John Jay Hall stood Butler Library, which I had seen the night before when I arrived. Above its arcade of Greek columns were inscribed the names of great writers, philosophers, and thinkers: Homer, Herodotus, Sophocles, Plato, Aristotle, Demosthenes, Cicero, Virgil,

Horace, Tacitus, Saint Augustine, Aquinas, Dante, Cervantes, Shakespeare, Milton, Voltaire, and Goethe. I was proud to recognize most of the names and to have read some of their works in college. For my philosophy course I had written an essay on the "Allegory of the Cave" in Plato's *Republic*, in which I compared the prisoners—who were facing a blank wall in a dark cave and chained to the floor—with my family and other migrant workers whose daily struggles simply to put food on their tables kept them from turning their lives around. I identified with the prisoner who managed to escape and help others break free. Now that I was at Columbia, I felt an even stronger affinity with that prisoner and a desire to use my education somehow to help liberate migrant workers.

As I cut across the red-brick College Walk, which served as a public pathway between Broadway and Amsterdam Avenue, and climbed a long flight of granite steps to an upper terrace, I was struck by the beauty of a large, imposing statue. It was of Minerva, the Roman goddess of poetry and wisdom. She was dressed in an academic gown, wearing a crown, and regally sitting on a throne with an open book on her lap and both arms outstretched. In her right arm she held a scepter. Farther up the stairs, on the top terrace, was Low Memorial Library, which served as the main library until 1934 and was now the administrative center of the university. I sat on the stairs overlooking the entire center of the campus quad and began thinking about my alma mater and its Spanish colonial architecture. I missed attending Mass at the Mission Church in the middle of campus and seeing the red-tiled buildings, two and three stories high, and ironwork and gardens with lush green lawns, palm and olive trees, and red and yellow and white roses.

I returned to my room, listened to the radio for a while, and got ready for the Woodrow Wilson reception. I put on my light green suit and clip-on tie that Father O'Neill, a Jesuit priest and mentor, had purchased for me for my Fellowship finalists' interview at Stanford University during my senior year in college. I took the elevator down to the lounge on the first floor, where the reception was to take place. I was the first one to arrive. The elegant wood-paneled room—with dark ceiling beams and paneling and plush red carpet—was stunningly beautiful. Large oil paintings of statesmen from the Colonial period decorated the walls. A bronze bust of John Jay sat on a pedestal next to a piano. To the left of it was a large stone fireplace, and above the mantel a framed marble slab had an inscription in gold lettering that read "Hold fast to the spirit of youth. Let years to come do what they may."

The chatter of two men dressed in black pants and white shirts interrupted my thoughts. One pushed a small cart with wine bottles, napkins, teacups and saucers, and wine-glasses; the other one carried a round glass tray with small sandwiches. When I greeted them and offered to help, they politely refused. A few minutes later a steady stream of well-dressed Woodrow Wilson Fellows, mostly men, filled the room and quickly formed small groupings. The subtle sweet smell of the men's cologne clashed with the strong scent of my Old Spice. Those in my group sipped wine and talked about their academic achievements and interests, foreign travels and alma maters: Harvard, Yale, Princeton . . . I envied their self-confidence and was intimidated by their vast travel experiences in Europe and other parts of the world. Many wore Phi Beta Kappa lapel pins. I listened nervously, avoiding eye contact and feeling a dry, dusty taste in my throat. I felt as out of place as I did when I entered the first grade not knowing a word of English, even though I was six years old then and now twenty-three. Feeling awkward and uncertain about everything around me, I excused myself, eased my way out of the lounge, and dashed up to my room.

Outside the Gates

Two days after settling in, I nervously ventured out to explore New York City. As I exited the west gate on 116th Street and Broadway, an eruption of traffic noise filled the air and political flyers and newspapers tumbled on the pavement in warm, humid gusts of wind. At the Broadway–Seventh Avenue subway station just outside the gates I asked the attendant for directions to downtown.

"Get off at Forty-Second Street," he said.

I bought a subway token for fifteen cents, went through the turnstile, and patiently waited on the platform for the train. The hot, dimly lit station felt like an oven. Its white-tiled walls were grimy and covered with graffiti. A picture of Columbia was set in a small mosaic tile border in the middle of the wall. A distant light appeared in the tunnel as the train made its way to the station, traveling south. As it drew nearer, it made a deafening noise—clunking, rattling, banging. When it finally stopped, it hissed and squeaked. The doors quickly opened and closed and promptly opened again. At each stop,

garbled messages came over a loudspeaker and the train became increasingly crowded with passengers, many of whom
appeared tired and sad. Some kept their heads down, others
stared straight ahead, avoiding eye contact, and a few dozed.
Across from me sat an old, disheveled man who was reading
the *Daily News*. He wore a tattered T-shirt, scuffed boots, and
pants torn at the knees. He marked passages in the newspaper
with a pencil and mumbled something to himself. I caught his
eye, smiled, and said, "Hello." He appeared startled. Without
saying a word, he got up and moved. I glanced at a red cord
near the door and wondered what it was for. Then I remembered riding the city bus in Santa Clara, California, and having to pull on a string to notify the driver that I wanted to
get off at the next stop. Figuring that we were getting close
to Forty-Second Street, I stood up and pulled on the cord. A
screeching sound blasted through the grimy sliding windows,
and the yellow fluorescent lights blinked and dimmed. Everyone looked frightened, and so I became alarmed too. What
was going on? The door slammed open. A tall policeman
rushed in, examining the premises like a sniffing dog. He held
a club in his right hand and glanced in my direction.

"Is this Forty-Second Street?" I asked timidly.

"Next stop," he responded, annoyed as he rushed to the
next car. At that instant I realized that the train stopped only
at designated stations. After a few minutes the train jerked,
slid back slightly, and continued moving forward. I looked
at the red cord again more carefully and noticed a sign under

it that read EMERGENCY BRAKE. I dashed to the door panels sheepishly, waiting to get off at the next stop.

The Forty-Second Street station was packed with people scurrying to connecting trains. I had not seen so many people speaking different languages and wearing distinctive clothes since I took the oath, with many others, for my citizenship in San Francisco when I was a junior in college. Elbowing my way up the exit stairs, I found myself in Midtown Manhattan, looking up at tall buildings. The traffic noise was deafening and relentless. Sun rays fought skyscrapers to reach the grimy streets and sidewalks. Waves of pedestrians going in both directions rushed past me as though they were in a race. I felt as if I were in a whirlwind and quickly stepped aside, taking refuge in a theater entryway that was littered with trash and smelled of urine. Then I began walking at a fast pace along a stretch of run-down theaters, glancing at marquees with multicolored flashing neon lights advertising adult entertainment. In the doorways, men wearing shiny polyester shirts, pegged pants, and pointed shoes handed out flyers promoting pornographic films and live nude dancers. The whole area and the men associated with it fascinated and disgusted me at the same time. It reminded me of Tiger Town in Santa Maria, a rough neighborhood lined with run-down bars and liquor stores on the west side of town. The sidewalks were littered with cigarette butts, crushed cigarette packs, and broken beer bottles. On Sundays when I was in high school, I had washed the grimy windows and swept the sidewalks of every bar in

Santa Maria, but unlike these men on Forty-Second Street, for whom I had mixed feelings, the men in Tiger Town saddened me. They were mostly *braceros*, temporary young farm workers from Mexico who came to Tiger Town from the local farm labor camps on Sunday afternoons when work was scarce. They sat at the bar drinking beer and listening to *ranchera* music on the jukeboxes, trying to distract themselves from missing their families and homeland.

A few blocks up from Forty-Second Street I passed several music stores. Music by the Beatles, the Rolling Stones, the Mamas and the Papas, and other groups blasted through loudspeakers near the entrances. A large poster of Elvis Presley displayed in a window drew me into one of the stores. He had been my favorite singer ever since eighth grade, when I pantomimed his "Treat Me Like a Fool" in front of the class, hoping to be more accepted by my classmates, who were Elvis fanatics. I browsed through stacks of vinyl records and record albums. The album cover for *If You Can Believe Your Eyes and Ears* by the Mamas and the Papas struck me as funny. It featured the group in a bathroom, sitting in a bathtub, with a toilet in the corner. Then it made me sad, as it reminded me of our dilapidated army barrack in Bonetti Ranch, where my family lived when I was in high school and college. We bathed in a small round aluminum tub in a makeshift shed that my father built next to the barrack with discarded lumber we found in the city dump. Behind the barrack was the outhouse, which we shared with two other families.

I left the store, wandered east to Fifth Avenue, and headed north. Immediately I was struck by how different it was from Forty-Second Street. Wide and clean, it had well-dressed pedestrians who smelled of sweet perfume as they passed by. They wore clothes I had seen only in fashion magazines. Men and women crossed the wide avenue, their elegance bordering on arrogance. Expensive stores with French and Italian names lined the avenue: Gucci, Ferragamo, Louis Vuitton, Prada. Brooks Brothers was the only name familiar to me because a few of my college classmates bought clothes with that brand. I went into Saks Fifth Avenue, which was swirling with stylishly dressed shoppers, and browsed through the display cases full of neatly arranged jewelry. A pair of silver earrings in the shape of butterflies caught my eye. I leaned closer to look at them and gawked at the price. Who could possibly afford to buy things here? I thought of my mother buying my siblings and me clothes at secondhand stores and complaining about the high prices. I walked out of Saks feeling awkward and uncomfortable. When I got to Fifty-Ninth Street, I noticed fewer department stores and more residential buildings, bordered by Central Park. I passed old-style mansions and palacelike apartment houses. Most of them had canopied entrances and doormen dressed in black uniforms. I glanced up at a lavish apartment building and saw sparrows building a nest in a small space beneath a third-floor window. One of them soared over my head and into the park. Instinctively, I ducked. The doorman, who must have been watching me, laughed and said, "It's an aggressive sparrow, don't you think?" I smiled and nodded in agreement. "Have a good day," he said.

"Thanks. You, too." I ran across the street and entered Central Park.

The park looked like a huge forest, a haven, with trees and lakes, ice rinks, tennis courts, baseball fields, and many playgrounds. I came upon a huge red-brick terrace on two levels that were united by staircases. Walking down to the lower level, I sat on a bench near a large fountain that featured a tall bronze angel standing above four cherubs. In front of it, a group of young hippies sat cross-legged in a circle, drinking and smoking marijuana. One of them strummed a guitar and sang out of tune. A couple embraced and kissed many times. I wondered what it would feel like to be so uninhibited. Like my parents, I never displayed affection in public. My father seldom expressed it in our home. I continued strolling on one of several serpentine walkways that interlaced the park. Passersby gave me the peace sign and a smile. Along the path were broken benches and rocks full of graffiti. Scribbled on a large smooth rock was "Make the Pigs Pay" and "Make Love, Not War." The sight of a homeless man lying next to it enveloped me in sadness. He was dark, emaciated, and unshaven, with dirty pants and shirt. His face was sewn with vertical wrinkles. I reached into my pocket and gave him the small change I had. I did not know what else to do.

"God bless you, brother," he uttered. Suddenly I felt depressed and tired. I left the park, took the subway back home, and panicked when I exited the station and didn't see the entrance gates to Columbia. I hurried back down. The man in the token booth took one look at my face and guessed my mistake.

"This isn't Broadway," he said. I had mistakenly boarded the wrong train and ended up on 116th Street and Lenox Avenue, which is on the East Side of Manhattan. I was in Harlem. He told me to take the subway back down to Forty-Second Street, then the shuttle, then the West Side train uptown. By the time I got home, I was exhausted.

The next morning I woke up late and tired, replaying in my mind what I had seen and learned the day before. The city seemed cold, distant, and impersonal but also full of life and stark, fascinating contrasts.

The Breakup

A few days after I arrived at Columbia, I received a letter from Laura that devastated me. It was in response to a letter I had written to her two days before leaving, after having worked all summer for the Southern Counties Gas Company of California. Mine was an emotional letter in which, for the first time, I told her that I loved her. I felt sad and insecure about our relationship when I wrote it, for I would not be able to see her for almost twelve months.

Laura and I had begun our relationship three years earlier, when we were undergraduate students at the University of Santa Clara, both majoring in Spanish studies. I was a sophomore; she was a freshman. We met for the first time in a survey of Latin American literature course. The moment I saw Laura, with her beautiful large brown eyes and high forehead and broad smile, I was attracted to her. She impressed me and everyone else, including the professor, by her intelligent and insightful analyses of literature, even though she was the only nonnative speaker in the class. Fate had it and it was my luck that we ended up working together in the language lab and sharing childhood experiences after closing hours. She told me stories about her Italian immigrant ancestors.

At the age of sixteen her maternal grandfather, Arrigo Descalzi, left his hometown in Sestre Levante, went through Ellis Island, and made his way to California, where he began selling vegetables from a horse-drawn wagon. He fell in love with and married Caterina Zunino, who also came from Italy and worked as a chambermaid in San Francisco. The whole family, including Laura's mother and father, spoke Italian at home. Laura was as proud of her heritage as I was of mine. On one occasion I even confessed to her that I was born in Mexico and that my family and I had crossed the border illegally when I was four years old. Her acceptance freed me from the secret that had haunted me for many years. Over time, I developed a deep affection for her and learned to trust her.

You need time to yourself, without any distractions, she wrote. *You should take advantage of all the opportunities Columbia and New York have to offer. I don't want you to take your mind off your studies and be thinking about the girl you left behind. I don't want to be a distraction to your work. . . .* My hands began to tremble as I read on. *It pains me to end my relationship with you but it's the best thing to do for you, for both of us.*

Laura was cautious and thoughtful about expressing her opinions and feelings, so I knew she meant every word. My eyes welled up and my chest tightened. I imagined seeing her in the same yellow dress she often wore in college. At that moment I wanted to enter her mind and open her soul wide to convince her not to break up with me. Her unselfishness made me love her even more. The muscles in my neck began to hurt. My throat ached and my temples were throbbing. The thought of not seeing her ever again, not hearing her voice, not communicating with her was inconceivable to me. I felt as if someone had cut out my heart. To drive away the pain, I rushed out of my room in a daze and wandered aimlessly through streets in the Upper West Side of Manhattan, wearing myself out. *Time heals all wounds*, I thought, trying to convince myself that the ache in my heart would eventually go away.

For the next couple of days I tried to answer Laura's letter, but each time I sat at my desk to write, I could not; my feelings ruled my mind. Late one afternoon after taking a long walk along Riverside Drive, which runs parallel to the Hudson River, I felt calm enough to think clearly and finally put into words what I needed to say. I hurried back to my room and began to write. It took all the strength I had not to express my true feelings about her breaking up with me. I knew that if I told her how heartbroken I was, she would feel sorrow. And, selfishly, I was too proud to plead with her to change her mind. *I have started this letter four times and I still don't know how to begin*, I wrote. I had a hard time keeping my hand steady. *I received your letter last Friday and I must have read it ten times. . . . Laura, I want to thank you for telling me what you did. I am glad you had more sense than I did to say it.*

My eyes welled and my throat tightened. I took a deep breath and continued. *Well, I too enjoyed having known you. I learned a lot from you. I feel that I am a better person for having experienced part of my life with you. . . . I don't know how to end this letter. I guess the best way is to wish you happiness and the best of everything.* I reread the letter, signed it, folded it carefully, and put it in an envelope. Two days later I mailed it, feeling sick. My heart pounded with impatience for time to pass.

First Encounters

The morning after the day I arrived, I was scheduled to meet with Professor James Shearer, chairman of the Graduate Spanish Department, for academic advice. I made my way to Philosophy Hall, an eight-story red-brick building built in 1910, the year my father was born. It had an arched entryway, with heavy beveled-glass double doors and wrought iron window screens. A large bronze sculpture in front of the building depicted a man crouching, his hand to his chin and his right elbow to his left knee. I had no idea whom the statue represented or who the artist was until I read an inscription at the base of it: "*The Thinker* by Auguste Rodin." While I was admiring it, a small black dog came up from behind me and began barking incessantly at the statue, circling it several times, wagging its tail, and then running away.

Inside the lobby I checked the directory to verify Professor Shearer's office number: 301. I climbed the worn marble steps to the third floor and nervously knocked on his door, which was ajar.

"Come in," he said in a raspy voice. He was sitting behind a majestic wooden desk and smoking a smooth curved pipe. As I entered, he placed it on a silver ashtray, greeted me, and asked me to sit down. He remained seated. I went up to him, introduced myself, and shook his hand. Then I sat down in a dark red leather chair facing him. He was a slender, distinguished-looking elderly man dressed in a tan tweed coat, dark brown slacks, and a striped bow tie. His face had a look of granite chiseled by experience and knowledge. His office, three times the size of my dorm room, had dark paneled walls, a high ceiling, and two large arched windows. The shelves behind his neat desk were filled with books. After looking at my record, he suggested that I enroll in fifteen semester units: Advanced Expression and Style, Spanish American Literature, The Middle Ages in Spain, Mexican Revolution Literature, and Don Quijote de la Mancha. Then, like a recording, he explained the requirements for the M.A. and Ph.D.

Before going on for a doctorate, I had to complete a master's degree—which required thirty semester graduate units—pass written and oral examinations, and write a thesis. For the Ph.D. I had to complete thirty semester units beyond the master's, pass comprehensive written and oral exams, have a reading knowledge of Latin and French, and write a book-length dissertation on an original research topic.

By the time he finished, my hands were sweaty, my heart pounding. "Do you have any questions?" he asked, picking up his pipe and taking a puff.

"About how long does it take to finish the doctorate?" I asked, wiping my hands on my lap.

"My opinion is that no one should complete it in less than ten years." My heart dropped to my stomach. "However, the current administration expects us to have students finish in six or seven years." I felt some relief and silently thanked the administration. "As far as I am concerned," he added, "you do not exist for us until you pass the Ph.D. comprehensive exams." I expected him to laugh, to tell me that he was joking. He kept a straight face. I feigned a smile and fidgeted. "Do you have any further questions?" he asked. Before I had time to respond, he quickly added, "Fine, then." He stood up and grabbed a small stack of papers stapled together on his desk and handed them to me. "Here's the reading list for the master's degree," he said. "I must run off to a meeting." His abruptness took me by surprise. I followed him out of the office and moved to the side as he slammed the door behind us and locked it.

"Thank you. It was a pleasure meeting you," I said.

"Likewise. Good luck!" he responded. His tall, slender body slipped away like a shadow.

I returned to my room, feeling worried and disappointed but, most of all, disrespected. I sat at my desk and read through the ten-page single-space reading list for the M.A. degree, which covered Spanish Peninsular and Latin American literature and literary criticism. Even though I was familiar with many of the titles and authors, my worry and disappointment turned into fear when I discovered that I had read only a few of the works. I said a prayer to the Virgen de Guadalupe, took the notebook from my desk drawer, and again, to give me courage, began reading notes I had written about my childhood.

I read the one about Torito, my baby brother, who contracted a serious illness during the time we lived in Tent City, a migrant camp in Santa Maria. He was a few months old when he began suffering from convulsions and diarrhea. My parents gave him mint tea and consulted a *curandera* folk healer, who rubbed raw eggs on his stomach. When he got worse, my parents rushed him to the county hospital even though they had no money to pay for medical care. The doctor told my parents that Torito was going to die, but they refused to believe him. They brought Torito home, and our whole family prayed every day to El Santo Niño de Atocha, the little baby Jesus, until my brother got well.

Hearing a soft knock, I placed my notebook back in the drawer and opened the door. A graduate student I had seen a couple of times in the hallway stood before me. He was of medium height, somewhat stout, with straight jet-black hair and bangs.

"Hi, I'm Phillip Andrews, your neighbor from across the hall," he said, smiling. I introduced myself and asked him to come in. He sat at my desk, I on the edge of the bed. "Weren't you at the Woodrow Wilson reception a couple of days ago?" he asked.

"I was . . ."

"Right. I thought I saw you there. What was your impression of Jacques Barzun's welcoming remarks?" Jacques Barzun was the dean of the graduate school, dean of faculties, and provost.

"I must have left before he spoke," I said. "I wasn't feeling well."

"It's unfortunate," Phillip said. "He's quite an impressive intellectual historian. I've read several of his writings. His book *The French Race* has been particularly useful in my own research on the failures and successes of Breton nationalism. Are you familiar with any of his works?" Phillip had a mischievous and humorous air about his eyes and large mouth. I felt uneasy, uncertain why he was asking me.

"No. My field isn't history," I said, trying to justify my ignorance. "It's Spanish—Latin American literature, actually."

"I am fascinated by Jorge Luis Borges and Cervantes. In fact, *Don Quijote* is next on my reading list," he said.

"I am taking a class on *Don Quijote* this semester," I said, feeling more at ease. Remembering my first meeting with the chairman of Spanish Department, I made a face.

"You don't seem enthusiastic about the course," he said, looking perplexed. I told him about my experience with James Shearer and how I felt disrespected.

He laughed and said sympathetically, "Don't take it personally. Many professors here treat students like that."

I felt some relief but even more disappointed.

During the course of our conversation I learned that Phillip had graduated Phi Beta Kappa from the University of Michigan two years before I graduated from the University of Santa Clara. He had received a Woodrow Wilson Fellowship to work on his doctorate in European history at Stanford University and was spending the fall semester at Columbia doing research under a Ford Foundation Fellowship.

From that day on, Phillip and I would get together periodically on weekends during study breaks in his room or mine. I preferred meeting in his room because I could look out his window and see the main campus, which was a magnet for protestors, curious spectators, hippies, dogs, folksingers, and tourists. Every time I entered his room, Phillip would be listening to classical music on the radio and reading either *The New York Times* or a novel. In the beginning, our conversations were mostly one-sided: Phillip doing the talking and I the listening. I did not mind, because I was learning a lot about different topics, especially politics. He talked fast, one thought colliding with the next; his razor-sharp mind bubbled over with information on any subject, or so it seemed.

One day I saw him at his desk sorting perforated yellow rectangular cards that had round corners. When I asked him what they were, he explained that they were IBM cards in which he stored research data, and he eagerly told me about his study of the Bretons, an ethnic group in France. "The French considered them dimwitted and primitive," he said, shaking his head. "This was especially true during the eighteenth to nineteenth centuries. Consequently, many Bretons felt shameful about their native heritage and native tongue." His voice became agitated as he continued. "Because of this shame, many parents didn't teach their children to speak their native tongue, only French."

"This was my own experience growing up," I said. "My older brother and I were punished in school if we spoke Spanish, even though it was the only language we knew, and some of the kids made fun of us and other Mexicans. They called us wetbacks and greasers. Some of my classmates in high school and college were ashamed of being Mexican." Anticipating Phillip's question about how I felt, I quickly added, "It was painful and humiliating, but I have always been proud of my heritage. My father insisted on it."

"Good for you. And your father!" Phillip stared at me with a frown, his eyes intense, as if what he was about to say was deeply felt.

"Tragically, we live in a racist society that fails to live up to its values and ideals of freedom and equality . . ." He paused, looked out the window, and continued as though he were thinking out loud. "Our country is in a state of degradation. The words 'All men are created equal' ring hollow when we witness racism and bigotry, particularly in the South." He threw up his hands and added, "I am disillusioned."

I had to memorize and recite those same words from the Declaration of Independence to my eighth grade English and social studies teacher the same day the *migra* came into the classroom and took me into custody. After spending nine long years working in the fields and living in constant fear of being caught, we were deported to Mexico.

"I am disappointed, Phillip, but not disillusioned," I responded. "In spite of all the problems in our country, there are many good people who are compassionate and willing to help each other." I thought of how lucky my family and I were to come back to the United States legally, thanks to Ito, a Japanese sharecropper for whom we picked strawberries. He sponsored us and loaned us money.

"But our country is not governed by good people," he said. "It's run by greedy corporations who buy and manipulate politicians to enact laws that favor the wealthy. We don't have a government of the people for the people."

"What about President Johnson's War on Poverty and the Civil Rights Act?" I countered. "In my mind he is a good person, a good leader." I learned from a Jesuit in college that a good leader is one who sees a need to be filled, enlists the aid of others, and sets about filling it in the best way he can, without compromising his integrity.

"The Great Society social reforms were initiated by President Kennedy, not Johnson. Johnson is a warmonger; he is using the money earmarked for those programs to finance the Vietnam War. How is that integrity? I am telling you, our government leaders are corrupt. I've lost hope."

I did not continue to argue with him, because he was so much more knowledgeable and articulate than I was about everything. I left his room feeling inadequate.

Several days later, on a Saturday afternoon, Phillip came by unexpectedly to say hello while I was listing to music and tidying up my room. I turned off the radio and offered him the seat at my desk. I stood by the door, facing him.

"I needed a break," he said. "It's been a busy week."

"For me, too."

He glanced at the card of the Virgen de Guadalupe pinned on the side of my desk and asked me about it. I explained that it was the Virgin Mary who in 1531 appeared in a vision to Juan Diego, an Aztec convert to Christianity, near what is now Mexico City. "She holds a special place in my heart and in the life of my family and many other Mexicans. The pope canonized Juan Diego and declared Our Lady of Guadalupe the patroness of the Americas," I added. "Whenever I feel down or need help, I pray to her."

"I was brought up Protestant, but unlike you, I no longer practice my religion. I've lost faith."

"Oh, no! A few days ago you told me you had lost hope, and now you're telling me that you have lost faith, too. You can't do that, Phillip." I felt sorry for him. "We can't lose faith and hope!" I said firmly. "My mother always told us that we should never lose hope, no matter how difficult life is. She said, 'If we lose hope and faith, *mijo*, what do we have left? A television set, a car, a house, if you're rich.'"

"By 'faith' your mother meant religious faith, I take it."

"Yes. She is very devout and wise."

"Your mother might be right," he said halfheartedly. "But how can anyone have hope and faith when we are confronted by the horrors of the gas ovens and concentration camps and atom bombs . . ." His voice grew louder and his face increasingly redder as he continued listing the ills of the United States and the world. When he paused to catch his breath, I excused myself, telling him that I needed to get some homework done at the library. After he left, I felt drained. In spite of our marked differences, though, Phillip and I enjoyed each other's company. He seemed amused by my inexperience living in a big city. As time went by, I felt more confident in contributing to our conversations, and eventually we became friends.

A Revolution

By the end of the day on Thursday of the first week of classes, I found myself staggering under an incredibly heavy load of assignments and surrounded by older graduate students who were far more knowledgeable and experienced and confident than I was. The majority of them came from Spanish-speaking countries and had attended prestigious universities in the United States and abroad. I felt intimidated and insecure about my academic preparation and aptitude. The fear of failing classes, losing my fellowship, and disappointing my family and the many people who made it possible for me to be at Columbia began to haunt me. *I must not let them down,* I told myself. I had had similar feelings during my freshman year in college, and I managed to deal with them by working extra hard and praying, drawing strength from my childhood experiences, and getting help from my professors. I would do the same here, I decided. The biggest challenge would be to find supportive and caring professors who, according to Phillip Andrews, were in short supply at Columbia.

Fortunately, Andrés Iduarte, who taught the Mexican Revolution Literature course, turned out to be one of those rare professors.

The class met on Fridays in the late afternoon on the second floor of Philosophy Hall. On the first day of class I arrived early and took a seat in the front row, near a window overlooking the statue of *The Thinker*. I placed my spiral notebook on my desk and nervously waited for the professor. As students entered the classroom, I mistakenly perceived a few of the older ones to be the teacher; they wore sport coats with ties and carried briefcases, but once each one occupied a desk, I knew they too were students.

After we waited ten minutes past the starting time, a man in his early sixties appeared at the door, looking like a portrait of a diplomat in a picture frame. He took off his hat, exposing a large, balding, perfectly round head, and introduced himself as Andrés Iduarte. He wore a double-breasted dark blue suit, white shirt, and red tie, and he carried a bulging black leather briefcase. He had broad shoulders, a protruding stomach, and small feet. He walked in, sat behind a small wooden table facing the class, and greeted us in a deep, raspy voice, *"¿Qué tal jóvenes?"* He unbuttoned his coat, reached into his briefcase, took out several thick leather-bound books, and piled them on the table next to his hat. He breathed heavily as he took attendance, made friendly comments on each of the names, and jotted down notes with a mechanical pencil on the class roster. He had long, slender hands that were full of life and energy. When he got to my name, he asked politely if I was ever referred to as Panchito, which is the nickname for Francisco.

"Yes, my family calls me by that name." I was nervous but pleased. He gave me a friendly smile and continued taking roll. When he was done, he began discussing in a thoughtful, dignified way, without being formal, the writers of the Mexican Revolution of 1910. One by one he picked up the volumes containing the complete works of each of the authors we were to read and made personal remarks about each one of them. Professor Iduarte described his relationship with Martín Luis Guzmán, Pancho Villa's private secretary, who wrote *Memorias de Pancho Villa* and *El águila y la serpiente*, The Eagle and the Serpent. Professor Iduarte and Guzmán were classmates at the Escuela Nacional Preparatoria, the oldest high school in Mexico City. He described his friendship with the artists Diego Rivera and Frida Khalo during the time he was director of the Instituto Nacional de Bellas Artes, the cultural center in Mexico City. He had been appointed to this post by Lázaro Cárdenas, the former president of Mexico. He also mentioned other artists, essayists, poets, intellectuals, and political figures from the period of the Revolution. His conversational tone and extensive knowledge of Mexican literature and culture were mesmerizing. What he was saying was for me like rain falling on dry ground.

"We have a couple of minutes left," he said, looking at his wristwatch. The two-hour class had gone so quickly! "Before

I forget," he added, "you are required to turn in a twenty-five- to thirty-page research paper at the end of the semester on any topic related to the literature of the Mexican Revolution." He stood up, buttoned his coat, and began placing the pile of books in his briefcase. I waited for all the students to leave before approaching him to ask what our daily assignments were. He caught my eye as he put on his hat.

"You have a question, Panchito?" I took a step closer and asked what I should read for the next class.

"Whatever you like," he said. Noticing my bewilderment, he was more specific. "You can start with *El Indio* by Gregorio López y Fuentes." I thanked him and left the classroom, boiling with excitement. For the first time, I had a teacher who was Mexican, who taught a class dealing with my native culture, a subject I had heard my father and other relatives talk about when I was a child.

I checked out *El Indio* from the Butler Library and became completely absorbed by it. Through the tragic love story of an Indian couple, the author explores the plight of the Indians in Mexico from the time of the Spanish conquest to the period immediately after the Revolution. The author details the subjugation of the Indian by the hierarchy of the church, the government, and *hacendados*—large landowners who robbed the Indians of their land, employed them, and treated them like slaves. Countless Indians died from smallpox and other diseases, which they attributed to a *brujo*, a man with supernatural evil powers.

Many aspects of the novel were real to me. My father, who was part Huichol Indian on his mother's side, was born the year the Mexican Revolution began and the year his father, Hilario, died. He grew up during the most violent and chaotic period of the war and spent most of his adolescence without a stable home, living here and there a few months at a time with his older brothers and sisters who were married. He never attended school, and by the time he was fifteen, he was on his own, working as a ranch hand in El Rancho Blanco. He told me about a ruthless *hacendado* in Jalisco, the state my family was from, who used his company store to keep my paternal grandfather and other peasants in a state of endless debt.

Like the Indians in the novel, my father believed in the force of *brujos*. He thought that his incessant headaches and bleeding ulcers were the result of his being hexed by someone evil in his native land. "I am cursed," he would say, clenching his teeth and burying his face in his leathery, scarred hands. The year we were deported, he sought help from a *curandera* in Mexico. He kept a glass half full of water under his bed to absorb evil spirits and alleged that he had seen La Llorona, the Weeping Woman. Out of respect, I never disputed his beliefs.

I returned to the library countless times to check out other novels of the Mexican Revolution. I liked climbing the wide marble staircase and seeing the Eisenhower portrait hanging in the stairwell, feeling the cool stone of the banisters, flipping through the card catalog, and browsing through the stacks. I was amazed at the number of novels about the Mexican Revolution and of the works written by Mexican authors.

Next I read *Los de abajo*, The Underdogs, by Mariano Azuela, in which the author depicts, in part, the horrors and dehumanizing effects of the Revolution. I recalled my Tía Chana, my father's older sister, relating a story about how the Federales as well as the revolutionaries committed atrocities.

"Los federales venían al ranchito montados a caballo y nos robaban lo poco que teníamos," she would tell us. *"Se llevaban las gallinas y, a veces, hasta las chicas más bonitas, a pura fuerza. Después venían los pobres revolucionarios, unos a pie, pocos a caballo, y trataban de hacer lo mismo, pero para ese entonces ya casi nada nos quedaba."* The Federales would ride on horseback into our village and rob us of the few things we had. They took our chickens and, sometimes, the prettiest girls, forcefully. Days later the poor revolutionaries would come, mostly on foot, a few on horseback, and try to do the same, but by then we had almost nothing left.

In the voices of the peasant characters in *Los de abajo* and other such novels of the Mexican Revolution, I heard the voices of my family and the community of my childhood.

Solitary Days

Many days had passed since I arrived at Columbia. It began to rain, and the rain turned into snow. Slowly I began to accept my new reality, confined mainly to the four walls of my room and Butler Library. I grew accustomed to going to classes, doing research, and reading. I would get lost in the novels of the Mexican Revolution and other class assignments until one or two in the morning. Sometimes I became so absorbed in my work that I would forget to eat until my aching, growling stomach and a growing sense of weakness reminded me. To avoid this, I made a sign saying DON'T FORGET TO EAT and tacked it above my desk. At the end of long days, to reward myself, I would walk to a deli near campus and have a cinnamon roll and a pint of milk. During the coldest days, when I did not want to go out and suffer the freezing weather, I would buy a packet of cheese and have a slice of it for a treat. I would wrap the packet in a paper bag and place it outside on the window ledge. Tying the bag to the radiator with a strong string prevented it from blowing away in heavy snowstorms.

The drudgery of my daily routine continued until December 21, the day the university closed for the Christmas holiday. Classes would resume after the new year, on January 3.

The day before the break, Phillip invited me to spend the holidays at his family's farm near Fulton, Michigan. He suggested taking the train the next morning. I thanked him and told him I would think about it and let him know that evening. I sat at my desk, looked out the window, and imagined myself riding the train, fleeing the monstrous concrete and asphalt city, and enjoying the scenery of the countryside along the way. I imagined the farm in Fulton looking like the dairy farms near Bonetti Ranch in Santa Maria, where cows roamed freely and grazed on emerald green alfalfa fields or rested under pepper trees. My daydreaming and the temptation to accept Phillip's invitation quickly ended when I glanced at the pile of books on my desk and considered the unfinished research papers. I decided to remain on campus and use the free time to study and write. Phillip was disappointed when I told him, but he understood my reasoning.

During the two-week Christmas break John Jay Hall was as quiet as a tomb. Most students had gone home to spend the holidays with their families and friends. I spent the time doing research in Butler Library, browsing through the musty-smelling stacks on the fifth and sixth floors, and checking out books and journals and hauling them to my room, where I stacked them neatly by categories throughout the room. I scanned them, taking copious notes on my portable typewriter and placing the notes in folders that corresponded to each of the final papers I was writing for my classes that first semester, which ended on January 21. My work occupied me and prevented me from being overtaken by loneliness.

As Christmas Day approached, I anxiously checked for mail, which was usually delivered mid-mornings to small lockable mailboxes that covered a whole wall of the lobby on the first floor of John Jay Hall. A few days before Christmas I received a brief letter from my father, which he dictated to my Tía Chana because he did not know how to write. It read:

Mi querido hijo, con tanto gusto recibí tu carta y el dinero que me mandaste. Desearía mandarte mi corazón para darte las gracias por todo lo que haces por mí. Dentro de mi alma nunca se me olvidará, y al recibir noticia que estás bien me da fuerzas y ánimo. Recibe muchos abrazos apretados de tu padre que te adora. Te deseo una feliz Navidad. My dear son, how happy it made me to receive your letter and the money you sent me. I wish I could send you my heart to thank you for all you have done for me. Deep in my soul, I'll never forget it. I feel strength and my spirit comes alive knowing that you are well. Receive many strong hugs from your father who loves you. I wish you a merry Christmas.

His words lifted my own spirit and touched me deeply,

but I worried about his health and wished he had said something about it. Fortunately, a couple of days later I got a greet-
ing card from my mother and younger siblings and a letter
from Roberto with news about our father and the rest of the
family. He had heard from Tía Chana that our father was still
recovering from his breakdown and that he appreciated the
money I had sent him. He used part of it to pay a *curandera*
who was attending to his back pain and headaches, using different herbs and folk medicine. *On a happier, note,* Roberto
wrote, *I have good news. I've finished my Associate of Arts degree
at Hancock and I was promoted to warehouse supervisor. Gracias
a Dios. Thank God.*

My brother had been working as a custodian for the Santa
Maria Elementary School District and taking night classes at
Hancock Community College. Darlene, his wife, was working part-time at Saint Mary's Hospital. She and Roberto
helped our mother and younger siblings economically and
gave them moral support. I smiled when I read about his
daughter, my favorite niece: *As I told you in my last letter, little
Jackie is doing well in first grade and enjoying school. She sends
you hugs and kisses.*

On Christmas Eve I began typing the final draft of my
paper on the portrayal of Emiliano Zapata in the novels of
the Mexican Revolution. I admired this revolutionary hero's
efforts and sacrifice to help emancipate the peasants and Indians in southern Mexico and lead them out of poverty. When

I finished, I gazed out the window. Snowflakes gently rested on the windowpane like tiny white butterflies and slid freely along the shiny surface.

I spent Christmas morning wrapped in a blanket, my head resting on my bent knees, thinking about the many Christmases that ended in disappointment for my siblings and me because our parents were too poor to buy us the gifts we wanted—and, in worst times, no gifts at all. Later, I went to Mass and wrapped myself in prayer and thoughts of my family when we were all together. This was the gift I now missed and yearned for the most.

Ups and Downs

The second week of January, during finals week, I delivered my research papers to my professors individually and attached to each paper a self-addressed postcard so that they could write my final grade on it and mail it back to me. This was the most expedient way to get grades. At ten o'clock on Monday morning I rushed downstairs to check my mailbox. Nothing. Tuesday, Wednesday, and Thursday brought the same disappointing results. On Friday morning I lingered around the lobby again, anxiously waiting. The mail finally came. I nervously inserted the key and opened the box. There they were. I quickly flipped through the postcards, looking at the letter grades. I received As in all my classes, except for a B-plus in the class on *Don Quixote*. My father's words, *"Vale la pena trabajar duro,"* it pays to work hard, flashed through my mind. Immediately, I wanted to call him, but he, like my mother, had no phone, and even if he had one, it was too expensive to call, so I hurried up the stairs, skipping two steps at a time, and knocked on Phillip's door to tell him. He was not in. I scribbled a note asking him to see me right away and slipped it under his door. I floated back to my room, thanked the Virgen de Guadalupe, and lay in bed listening to popular music on the radio. Slowly I began to relax. It was a feeling I had not had in a long time. Hours later a loud banging on my door startled me. I jumped out of bed and opened it. It was Phillip.

"What's the matter?" he asked, holding my note in his hand. He looked worried.

"Look at these," I said, holding up the grades.

"That's great!" he said, "This calls for a celebration!"

"That's what I was hoping you'd say." I glanced out the window. Snow was coming down hard. We bundled up and headed for the West End Bar and Grill, a popular gathering place for Columbia students on Broadway between 113th and 114th streets. The dimly lit pub had dark brown wood paneling and booths on both sides of a long bar stocked with partially full liquor bottles with multicolored labels. Being a historian and never missing an opportunity to show off his knowledge, Phillip explained that the bar had been a meeting place for many Beat Generation writers, including Allen Ginsberg and Jack Kerouac and Lucien Carr. I had heard only of Allen Ginsberg. Phillip went up to the bar and returned with a large pitcher of beer and two mugs.

"Here's to a successful end of the fall semester," he said,

pouring the beer into the thick glass mugs and filling them to the brim. He grabbed his, raised it, and added, "And to your grades."

"Thanks, Phillip. And to our friendship," I added. We drank and talked about politics and the escalation of American troops in Vietnam. As the pitcher emptied, I felt a wave of heat invade my body, and when I excused myself to go to the bathroom, I did not feel the gravity under my feet. I splashed cold water over my face and looked in the mirror. A chill ran down my spine when I remembered my father's voice warning me not to drink. I stumbled back to the booth and slowly slid onto the red vinyl seat. Phillip ordered another pitcher and refilled our mugs.

"To friendship and love," he slurred, lifting his mug and clumsily clicking mine. My mug tipped over and spilled onto the table. We laughed and simultaneously reached out and grabbed paper napkins from the chrome dispenser, wiping the table dry.

"You're a good friend, Phillip." I began to feel sad knowing that he was leaving to go back to Stanford at the end of the semester to finish his Ph.D. It was difficult to makes friends at Columbia. Graduate students in the Spanish Department lived off campus, and those who resided in John Jay Hall kept to themselves.

"Why the long face?" he asked.

"I was just thinking about how difficult it is to find and

keep good friends." I told him how the few friends I made in migrant camps or in school during the time my family followed the crops either moved away from me or I moved away from them. Every time this happened, I felt pain.

Phillip filled my empty beer mug and said, "It's worse finding and keeping love, don't you think . . . I mean, a friendship by definition has to be reciprocal, but not love. You can love someone, but that someone doesn't necessarily love you in return."

"You're right," I said, and told him about the relationship I had with Laura. I felt confident telling him about her.

"Do you still love her?" he asked.

"I do, even though she broke up with me and we haven't communicated in months. There isn't a day that goes by that I don't think about her."

"You know what they say: distance makes the heart grow fonder."

"In my case, distance has made my heart ache more and more." I feigned a smile. He laughed and took a drink. "What about you?" I asked. "Do you have a girlfriend back home?" He gulped, squirmed, and quickly excused himself to go the men's room. I knew I had touched a nerve and wondered why. When he returned, he seemed nervous and agitated. I was tempted to repeat my question, but knowing how uncomfortable it made him, I didn't pursue it. After a long silence he blurted out, "Well . . . why don't you call Laura and tell her you love her?"

His irritable tone surprised me. He must have read my face, because he softened it and said, "Call her."

I shook my head, saying no, even though deep inside I wanted to contact her. "What if she refuses to talk to me?"

"What if she doesn't? Call her and find out."

My feelings could not refute his logic. I dug deep inside for courage, and after a long silence I finally said, "Okay. I will."

"Great! Now that that's settled, let's head back."

I looked at my watch. It was two in the morning! "Eleven o'clock in California. Too late to call," I said. We both laughed.

Before we left the pub, I got two dollars' worth of quarters in change to make the telephone call.

We staggered through the snow back to John Jay. Phillip took the elevator up to his room, and I stayed behind to call Laura from one of the several pay phone booths inside Hartley Hall, which was adjacent to John Jay. I knew she was a resident assistant at the Villas, a complex of condominiums for senior-class women attending the University of Santa Clara. (I had jotted down her address from the "Dear John" letter she sent me and placed it in my wallet.) I sat inside the booth, closed the sliding glass door, placed the eight quarters on the metal shelf, and called the operator for information. She gave me the phone number listed for the Villas and informed me that it was a dollar twenty-five for the first three minutes. I nervously slipped five quarters into the slot and waited for the phone to ring. It rang several times before a girl finally answered. I gave her my name and asked to speak to Laura Facchini.

"I'll check to see if she's in," she said.

My heart raced faster and faster with each second. My hands trembled. I felt hot flashes and chills. I saw my face reflected on the glass door. *This is not me,* I thought; *this is not really happening.* I was about to hang up when I heard Laura's pleasant voice.

"Hello. What a nice surprise to hear from you."

I sighed with relief. I took a deep breath and explained why I was calling. My words tripped over each other as I rattled on about the grades I had received in my classes. When I stopped to catch my breath, she said, "Congratulations! I knew you could do it. How have you been?"

Quickly I told her about my experience the first time I took the subway. She laughed and then repeated the question.

"How are you?"

"I am fine," I said halfheartedly. I wanted to tell her that I was terribly lonely, that I missed her, but I could not tell her the truth. I did not wish to worry and alarm her and end the possibility of reestablishing our relationship. The telephone operator interrupted our conversation, indicating that I had fifteen seconds left and if I wished to continue, I needed to deposit another dollar and a quarter for the next three minutes. I deposited the remaining three quarters, hurriedly thanked the operator, and asked Laura if we could be in touch. To my surprise and joy she said yes. "I'll write to you tomorrow," I said.

We were disconnected. I leaned my head against the door and held the receiver to my ear for a while. Then I hung up the phone and staggered back to my room, replaying our conversation in my mind and getting increasingly upset with myself for boasting so much about my grades. I knew I would not be able to sleep, thinking about it. So I sat at my desk and wrote her a letter of apology for bragging and thanked her for listening to me. I slipped into bed, hugged the pillow, and fell asleep.

The next morning I woke with a bad headache, sluggishly got out of bed and splashed cold water on my face, and took two aspirins. I sat at the edge of the bed and noticed a letter on the floor, near the door. I opened it and glanced at the signature. It was from Phillip.

Francisco, I hope you and Laura reconnected over the phone last night. You are so fortunate to feel the way you do about her, which leads me to the point of this letter: I am sorry I did not answer you last night at the pub when you asked me if I had a girlfriend. I must respond to you even though it's difficult for me, as you must have surmised by my uneasiness when you posed the question. The fact is that I have never been attracted to women. However, there is someone special waiting for me at home. As you know, I am leaving this afternoon to catch the train back to Vicks-

burg, Michigan, *to spend the semester break with my family before*
returning to Stanford. I wish you well. Fondly, Phillip.

I quickly got dressed and went across the hall and knocked
on his door. He was surprised to see me. Holding the letter
in my hand, I said, "Thanks for confiding in me, Phillip. You
are a true friend."

"Sorry I didn't tell you earlier," he said, blushing and
turning away.

Feeling awkward and sensing that he did too, I quickly
added, "Let's have lunch together, and then I'll go with you
to the train station."

"I'd like that very much, thanks." He grabbed his bag and
backpack—he had shipped his books and other belongings
ahead of time—and we headed to the West End.

During lunch we talked about my phone call to Laura
and his and my plans for the future. His dream was to teach
European history at the University of Michigan so he could
be close to his family. "What about you?" he asked.

"I want to teach at a university, too, perhaps at the University of Santa Clara, my alma mater."

"Looks like we both want to return home."

We continued talking, with long periods of silence between topics. I had a feeling that he expected me to bring up
the subject of his letter, so I did. "Talking about home, I'd
like to meet your friend someday," I said.

He perked up, smiled, and said, "I'd like for you to meet

him, too." And with a light in his eyes he added, "Maybe someday you'll introduce me to Laura."

"God willing."

We took the subway from 116th Street to Pennsylvania Station in Midtown. Before he boarded the train, we hugged each other and said our last goodbye. Oblivious to the noise and the crowds, I stood alone on the dirty platform, waving to my friend through the window until the train left.

Harlem Next Door

Because of the bad experience I had with him at the start of the academic year, I dreaded having to meet with the chairman of the Spanish Department at the beginning of the second semester. But I had no choice. I had to get Professor Shearer's advice on and approval of the classes I wanted to take.

I dragged myself to his office in Philosophy Hall and knocked timidly on the door. "Come in," he said. The sound of his raspy voice brought chills up my spine. I opened the door slowly and poked my head in. He was sitting at his desk reading the newspaper and smoking a pipe. "Sit down. Let's see what you have," he said, putting down the newspaper and stretching out his right hand to grab the form in which I had listed a few courses I wished to take, among them Professor Iduarte's The Spanish American Essay, Professor Eugenio Florit's Spanish American Literature Since Modernism, and Professor Herbert S. Klein's Latin American Civilization, taught in the history department. "These classes are fine," he said, "but you should consider taking the course on Federico García Lorca." He proceeded to tell me that it would be taught by Lorca's brother, Francisco García Lorca—the first and only time he would teach it—and it was to be the last class of his teaching career. I had already taken the class on *Don Quixote* with him the first semester. I enrolled in the class on García Lorca because I interpreted the chairman's advice as a mandate. I was glad I did.

The class was held on the second floor of Hamilton Hall on Wednesdays from three to five. The classroom was small, with two entrances, twenty-five worn-out desks bolted to the floor, and a four-legged dark wooden table and chair placed on a platform reserved for the instructor. I took a seat in the back. The room quickly filled with students who applauded when Francisco García Lorca entered through the back door. He smiled and greeted several of them by name as he made his way to the front, carrying a thick leather-bound book. He placed it on the table, pulled out the chair, and sat down. His slim build, jet-black sparkling eyes, and thick grayish-black hair belied his age. I felt my self-confidence slowly fading as the students introduced themselves one by one. Most of them were far advanced in their studies for the Ph.D. at Columbia and were teaching at local colleges and universities. A few of them were political refugees from Cuba who had earned doctorates from the University of Havana, but their degrees were not recognized in the United States. I was the youngest in that class and the least experienced professionally, which was ironic because all through elementary, high school, and college I was the oldest in my classes—I had had to repeat first grade because I did not know English well enough.

Professor García Lorca, who taught classes entirely in Spanish, informed us that this was his last class. "I plan to enjoy it fully," he said almost gleefully. "I am going to talk about my older brother and his work, which is contained in this one volume." He grabbed the leather-bound book from the top of his desk, proudly showed it to us, and suggested that we obtain a copy from the library or purchase a copy at the Americas Bookstore in Manhattan. He appeared to be much more relaxed and open in this class than in the one he taught on *Don Quixote*. His jaw was not as tense, and he did not clench his teeth as often between sentences. He spent the first class talking about his brother and his family as a backdrop to his writings.

Federico García Lorca was born in 1898 in Fuente Vaqueros, a small town west of Granada in southern Spain. According to Professor Lorca, his brother was more absorbed by writing than by study. "Federico was a poor student," he told us, grinning. "He skipped classes frequently and was happiest writing, singing songs, reciting his poems."

When he mentioned that Federico had spent a year studying English at Columbia's School of General Studies at the beginning of the Great Depression in 1929, I listened with great interest, and even more so when he told us that Federico lived in John Jay Hall. Professor Lorca then read what his brother wrote about his dorm: "My room in John Jay is wonderful. It is on the twelfth floor of the dormitory, and I can see all the university buildings, the Hudson River and a distant vista of white and pink skyscrapers. On the right, spanning the horizon, is a great bridge under construction, of incredible grace and strength." I laughed to myself, thinking about my own unattractive room on the eighth floor of that same dormitory. At the end of the class the professor informed us that in lieu of a final we were to write a research paper on any aspect of his brother's work.

Immediately after class I rushed to Butler Library to check out Lorca's works. I was too late; they had been taken out the day before.

The next morning, I took the subway downtown and bought a one-volume copy of Federico García Lorca's complete works at the Americas Bookstore. Though used, it was expensive and the only one left. The beautiful edition was published in Spain and had a prologue by Jorge Guillén, a well-known Spanish poet and a member of the Generation of 1927, the same group of talented writers to which Lorca belonged.

On the way back on the subway I scanned the index of the two-thousand–page book. *Poeta en Nueva York*, on page 471, caught my eye. I tore off a piece of newspaper from a copy left on an empty seat and marked the page. Exiting the crowded, noisy subway station at 116th Street, I went straight to Butler Library to begin reading *Poeta en Nueva*

York. I discovered that Lorca had written it during his studies at Columbia from 1929 to 1930 and that this work was considered one of the most important collections of poetry he ever produced. I skimmed the pages, noting that it was divided into ten sections, using Roman numerals, and I became intrigued when I read the title of Section I: *"Poemas de la soledad en Columbia University."* Poems of Solitude at Columbia University. My enthusiasm quickly turned into frustration. The poems were a challenge to understand even after several careful and painstaking readings. Many of the images were strange: *"Asesinando por el cielo . . . dejaré crecer mis cabellos,"* Assassinated by the sky . . . I'll let my hair grow, *"Animalitos de cabeza rota,"* little animals with broken heads, *"mariposa ahogada en el tintero,"* butterfly drowned in the inkwell. Even though I knew that his poetry was classified as surrealistic, I worried that it was my own lack of ability to understand it.

The following Wednesday I went to class hoping that Professor Lorca would explain the poems. His explanations were helpful, but even he, by his own admission, had trouble making sense of some of the lines and indicated that literary critics did not always agree about the meaning of many of them. "I think that Federico did not know what he meant either," he said. "Seriously, if you have difficulty with certain passages, it's best not to worry about the exact meaning; concentrate on the images and their emotional power."

After many more readings and rereadings and class discussions, I understood *Poeta en Nueva York.* Federico García

Lorca felt lonely at Columbia and disconnected from the city, a feeling I could empathize with. I was drawn in by his long poem *"Oda al rey de Harlem,"* Ode to the King of Harlem, in which he explores the alienation and isolation of the blacks living in Harlem and their being subjected to racism and discrimination. I then read an interview with Lorca in 1933 in which he talks about blacks in the United States:

"Es indudable que ellos ejercen enorme influencia en Norte-America . . . son lo más spiritual y lo más delicado de aquel mundo. Porque creen, porque esperan, porque cantan y porque tienen una exquisita fe religiosa . . ." Undoubtedly, they exert enormous influence on North America . . . they are the most spiritual and most refined of that world. Because they believe, because they hope, because they sing and because they have an exquisite religious faith . . . .

Before coming to New York City, I knew hardly any blacks. There were only two in my high school class of 380 students and just as few in my college class of 579. I remembered them well, but the most memorable was Aldo Nelson, whom I met after my sophomore year in college. He was a young field supervisor working for the Southern Counties Gas Company of California. I was hired by the same company that summer to clean and paint gas meters throughout the central coast under his supervision.

One scorching late afternoon Aldo and I took a break at a coffee shop in Paso Robles, a small agricultural town about seventy miles north of Santa Maria. We parked the white company pickup truck in front, entered the shop, and sat at the counter next to each other. The waitress walked past us several times, looking the other way. After a long wait, Aldo got up and said, "Come on, let's go."

"Why?" I asked.

"I'll tell you later," he said, visibly upset.

I followed him, feeling confused. When we got into the truck, I asked him why we had to leave in such a hurry. He did not respond. After driving for several miles back to Santa Maria, he broke his silence.

"Didn't you notice that the waitress didn't want to serve us?"

"What do you mean?" I was still puzzled.

"It was obvious! She served other customers who came in after we did. She ignored us. Why? Because I am black. She's a racist!" he said angrily.

I felt stupid and embarrassed because I had been so oblivious. "Let's go back and complain!" I said.

"What for, to face more humiliation?" He shook his head and gripped the steering wheel with both hands.

"I understand how you feel," I said, placing my left hand lightly on his shoulder. I told him how Roberto and I had experienced discrimination from parents who forbade us to go out with their daughters because we were Mexican.

He gave me a soulful look and said, "Unfortunately, discrimination is worse for us blacks."

I did not disagree. I knew about and sympathized with the

struggle in the South to end racial segregation and violence against blacks and to secure their civil rights.

After remembering this incident and reading *Poeta en Nueva York* and the interview, I decided to see Harlem with my own eyes.

On a cloudy and chilly Sunday morning I bundled up and headed north on Broadway to 125th Street and then turned east. At the northeast corner of Lenox Avenue and 125th I stopped and gazed at a large abandoned building that held a giant billboard advertising Marlboro cigarettes. Columbia University loomed in the distance. As I continued walking, I had to sidestep cracked and uneven sidewalks and scattered chunks of concrete and trash. I was amazed at the absence of greenery and the number of blocks with crumbling buildings. Some dwellings were boarded up, or had the boards torn off, the windows and doors smashed and broken. They reminded me of the old army barrack my family had lived in. It too had broken windows and holes in the walls when we first occupied it.

I approached a long line of people, young and old, going into a brownstone townhouse that, to my surprise, turned out to be a Baptist church. I stood outside and listened to gospel music pouring through the front door, the angelic sounds filling the air. I went on to the next block and passed a number of stores and brownstones that served as places of worship—Baptist, Methodist, Episcopalian, and Roman Catholic. I saw a woman gazing out of a window on the second floor of another brownstone townhouse, and I wondered what she might be thinking. Several blocks later I came across a junkyard littered with garbage and abandoned cars, and children were playing baseball in the street, using a broken broomstick for a bat. The image of my younger siblings in tattered clothes flashed through my mind, and I felt my throat tighten. Across the street I saw a teenage girl cradling an infant in her arms, walking hurriedly past two disheveled men who sat on the front steps of a hollowed-out building playing cards and drinking from bottles hidden in brown paper bags. They would be drinking to forget their troubles, like the *braceros* in Tiger Town. I turned the corner and saw on the opposite side of the street a liquor store with steel shutters, five teenagers hanging out in front, joking and laughing. One of them caught my eye and yelled, "What the hell you doing here, white boy?" I was stunned. I had heard kids call me "chile stomper," "tamale wrapper," and "greaser," but never "white boy." When he and the other four swaggered toward me, I got scared and ran like a cat on fire. When I got to the end of the block, I looked over my shoulder to see if they were following me. To my relief, they were not. I stopped to catch my breath and headed back, taking a different route. On the way home, liquor stores seemed to pop up at every corner.

My walk through Harlem brought back memories my family living in dirt-floor tents or old garages without electricity and indoor plumbing, searching for clothes in the city dump and scavenging for food in garbage cans behind grocery stores. Blacks in Harlem lived in similar circumstances. Yet these inhuman conditions did not define them; nor did they define families like my own.

I returned to Harlem regularly to attend Mass on Sundays at Saint Charles Borromeo Church on 141st Street between Seventh and Eighth avenues, and each time I went, I gained a deeper understanding of Lorca's views on blacks and felt more and more in solidarity with them.

Choices Made

During the second semester, just when I was feeling that my life was more secure and less stressful, I received a letter from Columbia's financial aid office informing me that my fellowship application for financial assistance for the following year had been approved for tuition only. The fellowship did not include funding for living expenses or room and board. I depended on a living stipend to help not only me but also my family pay for rent and food. What would I do? Fortunately, Hans Rosenhaupt, director of the Woodrow Wilson National Fellowship Foundation, must have anticipated this problem because he had advised me in the fall to apply for admission to Stanford. *Stanford is better off with fellowship money than is Columbia*, he wrote. I waited anxiously to hear from Stanford.

On March 8, Stanford notified me that I had been admitted to their graduate division for work in the Department of Modern European Languages and offered me tuition, but for one year only. I panicked, and immediately called the Woodrow Wilson Foundation office and left a message for Mr. Rosenhaupt, explaining my dilemma. Two days later he sent me a letter telling me that the foundation would supplement the tuition fellowship at either Columbia or Stanford with a two-thousand-dollar living stipend, and he suggested that I accept Stanford's offer. He wrote: *Still another argument in favor of your going to Stanford: they have already invested in you, which is always a good sign of interest and augurs well for future support beyond the first year. As to the relative merits of the two departments I just couldn't say.*

I was ecstatic at the good news. But now I had to decide between continuing at Columbia or transferring to Stanford. My immediate reaction was to attend Stanford. I would be closer to my family and Laura. On the other hand, by the end of the spring semester at Columbia I would complete the course work for my M.A., and in the fall, I would begin my master's thesis under the direction of Andrés Iduarte, the Latin American literature specialist, for whom I had such high regard. I also hated the thought of having to move again and start over. I kept going back and forth and praying for a solution. I called Roberto and explained my dilemma. "We'd love for you to go to Stanford, so you can be closer to us, but you know more about these things than I do," he said. "Trust your instincts." I decided to call Laura for advice. I trusted her judgment too. Besides, she was indirectly responsible for my getting the Woodrow Wilson Fellowship and attending Columbia.

When the University of Santa Clara nominated me for a Woodrow Wilson Fellowship during my senior year, I felt honored but was convinced I didn't have a chance of receiving it. When I told Laura that I wasn't sure I should apply, that I did not have a chance of getting it, she said, "Of course you do! Why would the university nominate you if you didn't? If you don't apply, you won't get the fellowship for sure."

Because of her encouragement and confidence in me, I went ahead and filled out the lengthy application and submitted it. To my surprise, I made the regional finals, and after an extensive interview by a panel of three judges, I was notified by Hans Rosenhaupt that the national selection committee had awarded me a Woodrow Wilson Fellowship.

Laura and I had not spoken with each other since January, when I called her about my first-semester grades. Feeling nervous, I placed the call in the evening from a pay phone booth in Hartley Hall and waited impatiently for it to go through. When Laura answered, her sweet, tender voice put me completely at ease. As I was explaining the pros and cons of my dilemma, she politely interjected with questions and made comments that clarified my own thinking. When I finished, there was a long pause. Then she asked, "What's your inclination?"

I wanted to tell her that one of the benefits of going to Stanford was that I would be closer to her. However, I resisted because I knew from the experience of her breaking up with me what her reaction would be.

"If Stanford had guaranteed me funding every year until I completed the doctorate, I would go there," I responded.

"Too bad it didn't," she said sympathetically. "But in this case, you should make a decision based on what's in front of you. Will it take you longer to complete your doctorate at Columbia or at Stanford?"

"Probably at Stanford . . . Because at the end of this semester I will complete two residence units at Columbia, and these units don't transfer."

"So, what do you think is best?"

After a brief silence I responded, "I guess . . . it's better to stay at Columbia."

"It's pretty clear, isn't it?"

"I guess it is."

At the end of our brief conversation I thanked her for helping me think things through.

A few days later, after informing Hans Rosenhaupt of my decision and the reasons for making it, he wrote back: *After looking at all the possible advantages and disadvantages I finally conclude that you would indeed be best served by continuing at Columbia University.*

After reading his response, I immediately sent a letter to Laura.

I received the Woodrow Wilson Foundation letter of approval. The pressure is off! . . . And after we hung up the phone the other day, I thought of many, many more things I wanted to say, not important things, just little things I enjoy sharing with you.

My connection with Laura gave me a sense of self-confidence and relief from feeling lonely. I felt eager to establish a stronger bond with her, so as time passed, my letters and occasional phone calls to her became increasingly personal and intimate. But Laura reined me in. In one of her letters she wrote, *Don't hurry our relationship. Let it grow on its own and enjoy its beauty.* I knew she was right, but my heart was impatient.

At the end of May, Laura sent me her graduation picture and a long letter telling me her plans for next year. She was going to attend San Jose State University, beginning in the summer, to attain a teaching credential to teach Spanish in high school. She also mentioned that she had received honorable mention for the Saint Clare Medal, the highest honor given by the University of Santa Clara to a female student. I was not surprised. Laura worked very hard at everything she did and did it well.

Even though I had successfully completed my first year of graduate school, I felt I needed free time during the summer to study and read in preparation for the written and oral exams required for the master of arts degree. But I also needed to work full-time to help my family, as I had done every summer during high school and college. I applied to the Ford Foundation for a five-hundred-dollar summer fellowship to allow me to fly home and study and work part-time. I received the funding and now had to seek part-time employment. I wrote to the Southern Counties Gas Company of California, for whom I had worked the previous three summers, and was turned down. They did not hire part-time. I then contacted Mrs. Marian Hancock, an elegant, dignified, and generous lady who had hired me during Christmas break when I was a sophomore in college to deliver gifts to her friends who lived in Santa Maria and at Vandenberg Air Force Base, near Lompoc. She had given me a round gold-plated wristwatch for graduation. Within a week she wrote back, giving me the good news that her close friends Tollie and Marie Golmon had offered to hire me part-time to work in their small family printing business, Paramount Printing Company in San Jose. I accepted the job.

Even though I could not be with my family in Santa Maria that summer, I was happy to live near Laura, who attended summer school at San Jose State and worked part-time in the office of High Continental, a food-service company at the University of Santa Clara. *Things do happen for a reason*, I thought.

Laura and her friend shared a second-floor apartment on South Eighth Street in San Jose. With the Golmons' help, I found and rented a one-room apartment with kitchenette behind an old Victorian home on South Third Street, which was only five blocks from where Laura lived and a few blocks from San Jose State University's library, where I went every late afternoon after work.

I enjoyed working for the Golmons at Paramount Printing Company—five days a week, from eight in the morning to two in the afternoon. I answered calls and filled orders for clients throughout the Bay Area.

Marie Golmon was short and plump, in her early sixties. She had an angelic round face, pale skin, thin lips, light brown eyes, and short, black-tinted hair. Tollie Golmon, on the other hand, was tall and thin, in his late sixties. He had a mischievous smile, sun-bronzed skin, blue eyes, and gray hair. His body reminded me of Don Quijote. Marie and I worked side by side in the front office, and Tollie worked in the shop behind the office, supervising a crew of three pressmen. When things were slow in the front office, Tollie would take me to the shop and explain in great detail how the presses worked. "I'll show you the secrets of printing," he would say. Everyone who worked for them, including myself, felt like a member of their family.

In the early evenings, after work, Laura and I took long walks around the San Jose State campus and a nearby park. We talked about our families, our studies, and work, and it seemed that with every step we took, I felt closer to her. One day I even confessed to her that her reasons for ending our relationship made me love her even more. "I'm glad you told me," she said. "We have to be honest with each other and help each other grow. The breakup was painful for me, too."

Toward the end of the summer I knew in my heart that I wanted to marry her.

Before asking Laura, I took the bus home that weekend to

tell my mother and Roberto and Darlene how I felt. This was the third weekend I had visited my family that summer. They were not surprised when I told them. They had met Laura at my college graduation and knew that she and I had been good friends for two years before we started dating and that we had been going out all summer. "I expected it," Roberto said with glee in his eyes.

"She is a lovely girl, and smart," Darlene said, smiling from ear to ear.

"*Ella es linda y muy buena gente, mijo. Merecen casarse.*" She is beautiful and a very good person. You deserve to marry each other, my mother said.

"When do you plan to marry?" Roberto asked.

"I was thinking next summer. But . . . I am not sure I can afford it. Do you think I should wait?"

"If you wait until you can afford it, you'll never get married," Roberto said. "Look at Darlene and me. We got married without either of us having money. Her family was as poor as ours. But we worked hard and managed. We love and respect each other and have two beautiful girls . . . family . . . this is what matters, *familia*. So get engaged now and marry her next summer. It'll all work out, trust me."

"What about you, *Mamá*?" I asked. "Are you okay with it? I may not be able to help out as much."

"*Ay, mijo,*" my mother said. "*Todo se puede con la ayuda de Dios.*" Oh, son, everything is possible with God's help.

"*Mira*, Trampita and Torito are now both working. So don't worry about us!" My mother often slipped in and out of Spanish and English, as did my younger siblings.

Trampita was working as a janitor for Saint Mary's Catholic Church and attending Hancock College part-time at night; Torito, a senior in high school, worked part-time as a custodian for the Santa Maria School District; and Rorra, a freshman in high school, and Ruben, who was in the seventh grade, helped my mother pick strawberries on weekends during the harvest season, April through the end of September.

"*Gracias, Mamá*," I said.

I knew that Roberto and my mother were right. When I thanked them and said goodbye to them and my younger siblings, it was an emotional departure, as always. I would not see them again until the end of the next school year. I had just enough money to fly back to school, not to come home at Christmas. I would have to spend another Christmas away from my family.

On my last day of work, Marie and Tollie gave me a surprise farewell party. It, too, was an emotional parting. I told them how much I enjoyed and appreciated working for them. "You are like the son we never had," Tollie said. "We have two girls!" I was moved, and promised to keep in touch.

That evening I went over to Laura's apartment for dinner. She had invited me the day before during our long walk. I decided this was my opportunity to ask her to marry me. Looking radiant, she was waiting for me at the top of the stairs. Her roommate had gone out with friends that evening. I was tense, but after we had our meal with a glass of red wine, I felt more relaxed. Bracing my legs around the chair, I said, "What about next summer?" My nerves had gotten in the way. What I really meant to say was: What do you think about us getting married next summer?

"What about it?" she asked, giving me a perplexed look.

"I mean . . . Do you think we could spend the rest of our lives together?"

Her large brown eyes stared at me in surprise. "Are you proposing to me?"

"Yes, I guess I am."

"You guess . . ?"

I often said "I guess" to begin or end a sentence in answering questions, especially when I felt nervous. Father O'Neill, a Jesuit priest, had even told me in college to avoid its use because it communicated weakness or lack of self-confidence.

I cleared my throat and said, "I'm very sure."

Her eyes welled up, and she smiled. She thought for a minute and said, "We have known each other now for four years, and I feel we know each other well. We share many interests and enjoy each other's company, talking and listening to each other."

"We do," I said. "We have the same religious beliefs and values . . ."

"And many, many things in common," she said. "We have simple wants; we respect and trust each other; we love children . . ."

"Is that a yes?" I asked, feeling anxious.

"Of course," she said. "Our long friendship has turned into a loving relationship." She extended her right hand and placed it on mine. We stood up, moved away from the table, and hugged each other and kissed. Then we started discussing possible wedding dates and decided on August 17. It was an evening of happiness, gratitude, and joy that I would never forget.

That weekend Laura and I went to her parents' home in San Carlos to tell her mother and father about our decision to get married. I had met them during my senior year in college when they visited Laura at the university, but I had never been to their home.

Laura's father, Oreste, was a wine salesman for Almaden Vineyards, and her stepmother, Wanda, ran a liquor store. Laura's mother, Gemma, had died at the age of thirty-two from multiple sclerosis when Laura was nine years old and her younger sister, Lynn, was seven. Wanda's first husband had died of colon cancer, leaving her with two young children, Marsha and Bradley. Oreste and Wanda married and formed a new family of six. Laura and Lynn considered Wanda as their mother.

Wanda, a stylish and graceful lady, answered the door and welcomed us. Oreste sat in the living room in an easy chair, his legs crossed, reading the newspaper. His thick, silvery white hair, combed back and receding, made him look older than his early fifties. He said hello, grinned, and asked me to have a seat on the wide sofa facing him. I could feel my heart pounding. Laura accompanied Wanda to the kitchen to make coffee. Oreste continued reading the paper. Mustering all the courage I had, I broke the long silence. "Mr. Facchini . . ."

"Yes," he said, flipping the page of the newspaper and peering over it to see me.

"I . . . I want to ask you for Laura's hand in marriage." My mouth felt dry. I wiped my sweaty hands on the side of my pants, glanced at the knickknacks on the end table, and looked at him.

"Well, this is a surprise," he responded, folding the newspaper in half and placing it on his lap. His large hazel eyes were intense and penetrating.

"I mean, next summer," I quickly added, thinking this would make it easier for him to say yes.

"How much money do you have saved?"

It was a question I had not anticipated. I quickly calculated: two hundred dollars left from the Ford Foundation summer grant and about six hundred dollars saved from working at Paramount Printing Company. "I guess I have about eight hundred dollars," I said. He gulped and glared at me. Did he think I was being disrespectful, playing a joke on him? "I'll have more money saved by next summer," I added.

Laura and Wanda entered the room, interrupting our

conversation. Wanda carried a plate of assorted cookies and Laura a small tray with cups and a carafe of coffee. "Isn't it wonderful, Orey," she said. "Laura just told me the good news." He feigned a smile and looked sadly at Laura as she poured him cup of coffee.

"Dad, you don't need to worry," she said tenderly. "Francisco and I will be okay."

"You have my consent," he said grudgingly, "but don't expect any help from us."

I was happy for his approval but felt offended. "Thank you, Mr. Facchini," I said. "I don't expect any help. I'll have my master's degree by the time we get married and will get a job teaching. I also have a fellowship that pays for my tuition and living expenses." *Even if I were dying of thirst*, I thought, *I wouldn't ask him for a glass of water.*

"And by then I'll be done with my teaching credential at Santa Clara and will get a teaching job in New York while he finishes his Ph.D. And once he's done, we'll come home to California," Laura said.

"Sounds like you both have thought this all out," Wanda said. "It will be fun planning the wedding, and we have a whole year to do it!"

"Unfortunately, Francisco won't be here," Laura said, giving me a sorrowful look. Her voice cracked.

My throat tightened. "But we'll be writing to each other, and you can keep me informed."

Laura's father remained silent. He picked up the newspaper, excused himself, and left the room.

Laura and I left her home feeling happy and relieved that her parents had given us their approval, but I was embarrassed because I didn't have an engagement ring to give her. I didn't mention it to her, and she didn't ask. I figured she knew that I couldn't afford to buy her one then.

I called Roberto that evening to share my joy with my family. Roberto and Darlene were excited. "I know you and Laura will have a happy marriage," my brother said. "You're perfect for each other. I'll tell Mom and the rest of the family." His words comforted me and convinced me even more that Laura and I had made the right decision.

When I left for Columbia at the end of the summer, I was heartbroken. Leaving Laura and my family behind again for another year was as painful as yanking out a fingernail, and for days I felt an ache in my chest.

A Surprise

I took a redeye flight on American Airlines from San Francisco to New York City to begin my second year of graduate school. I had a miserable cold and a pounding headache, and having to be apart from my family and Laura for another year weighed on my heart. I took two aspirins, fell asleep, and had what was for me a frequently recurring dream in which I was extremely tired from being on my knees, picking strawberries alongside Roberto, my father, and other farm workers. Every time I tried to get up, I would collapse. My legs and arms felt like lead. I pleaded for help, but no one could hear me. The jolt of the airplane hitting the runway and groaning woke me up. It was 6:15 in the morning. I glanced out the window; the day was cloudy and gloomy. I picked up my suitcase, boarded a shuttle bus to the East Side Airlines Terminal on Thirty-seventh Street, and took the subway up to Columbia. I checked in at the housing office in Hartley Hall and was assigned to room 817 in John Jay.

After reclaiming my belongings, which I had stored in the

basement of the residence hall for the summer, I carried them to the elevator and up to my room. The old, soiled green carpet in the hallway had been replaced with a dark blue one, and remnants of it were piled in the corner by the elevator. I picked up a large piece of carpet to use as a mat by the side of my bed, reminding me of how my family built a floor in our tent when we lived in Tent City by making frequent trips to the city dump to look for discarded lumber. My new dorm room was exactly the same size as the one I had the previous year except this one faced the campus, with a view of the main quad and the west corner of Hamilton Hall.

Even though my room was comfortable, I decided to search for a less expensive place to live, one that had cooking facilities, so that I could afford to buy Laura an engagement ring and help my family, using money from my fellowship living stipend. I found a notice on a bulletin board inside Butler Library advertising a furnished room with kitchen privileges, one block from Columbia, for sixteen dollars a week. Unfortunately, when I got there, the elderly couple who owned the apartment had already rented it. I felt discouraged and stopped looking when I discovered that there was a penalty fee of seventy-five dollars for breaking the contract with the university housing office. Opting to stay in John Jay Hall, and knowing that I would be breaking dorm rules, I went out and bought a single-burner electric hot plate, a skillet, a can opener, utensils, and a couple of dishes so that I could cook and eat three meals a day in my room. (The year before, I had limited myself to two meals a day: a cold cereal breakfast in my room and dinner in the school cafeteria.)

The third day, after I had settled in, I bought some groceries and tried my chef skills. I closed the door and opened the window to air out the room. Then I chopped some onions, mixed them with ground beef and canned corn, and cooked the blend in the small frying pan. As I was preparing my meal, I sadly remembered my mother cooking *verdolagas*, wild spinach, outside our tent on a makeshift stove using rocks and a *comal*, flat frying pan, when we first lived in Tent City.

I was enjoying my dinner when I heard a soft knock on my door. I quickly gathered my cooking gear, hid it in the closet, and opened the door. To my relief, it was my next-door neighbor, Steve Winter, whom I had met the first day. He was short and slim, with dark, curly hair, brown eyes, and delicate hands with long, slender fingers. He spoke as if he were chewing his words.

"Hi, mate," he said. "It smells bloody good. What are ya cooking?" The odor of my delicious meal had obviously made its way to the hallway and into his room. When I explained what I was doing and why, he sympathized with me and told me that he, too, was on a tight budget and had borrowed money to study for his master's degree in architecture at Columbia. He went on to say that after graduating from the University of Sydney with a bachelor's degree in architecture, he left home and moved to London, where he shared an apartment with his older sister and her boyfriend for a year. Since we both needed to economize, I invited him to join me in my venture and gave him a taste of what I had cooked. "This sloppy joe tastes good, but let's add tomato sauce next time," he said. We both laughed and agreed to share the cooking and cleaning and to share expenses fifty-fifty.

Now I could afford to buy Laura an engagement ring. The next morning, I went to Columbia's bookstore and asked a clerk where I might find bargains on diamond rings. She suggested taking the subway to Canal Street in lower Manhattan. "It's the jewelry trade center," she said.

Canal Street reminded me of Midtown. It was lined with storefront jewelry stores and sidewalk stalls, crowded with tourists who jostled for space and bargained with vendors over handbags, perfumes, and sparkly watches. I went in and out of various stores, looking at hundreds of diamond rings and becoming increasingly confused. Many of them looked exactly the same, yet they differed in price. At each store, I was given a hard sell; none of the clerks seemed honest. Discouraged and tired, I continued my search until I came upon C. Scholar Diamond Co., Inc. It covered two storefronts on 70–72 Bowery, which intersected with Canal Street. Mr. Scholar, the owner, greeted me, and after I told him I was looking for an engagement ring, he pulled out a tray of diamond rings, neatly arranged in rows, from under a display case, placing it on the counter. He adjusted his black velvet *kippah* and proceeded to explain to me that the value of diamonds depended on size, clarity, color, and cut. "How much are you thinking of spending?" he asked.

"Between one hundred and two hundred dollars," I said.

He smiled, took out another tray, picked out a beautiful diamond with a simple setting, and handed it to me. *Laura would love this one*, I thought.

"This is the finest ring we have in your price range," he said, "It's a fine cut, seven-tenths carat, and goes for two hundred and thirty-three dollars, including tax. It's really a bargain."

"What about its clarity?" I asked, noticing that he had not mentioned it.

He examined it with his loupe magnifying glass. "It has a small occlusion, an imperfection," he said, "but it's not visible to the eye."

"May I look at it?" I asked. He handed me the magnifying glass and the ring. I inspected it carefully and could see a tiny thin dark line cutting across the diamond.

"Like I said, it's not visible to the eye," he repeated.

I told him I was interested in buying it but not sure it was worth that price. He suggested that I pay for it and have it appraised at M. Simpson, Inc., a diamond and jewelry appraiser on Canal Street. "If it's appraised for less than what you paid, come back and I'll make up the difference, or you can return it and I'll give you your money back." I bought the ring and took it to 141 Canal Street, where M. Simpson, the owner, appraised it for $375. He gave me an official certificate of appraisal, which he had signed.

When I returned home, I read the disclaimer in fine print at the bottom of the certificate: "No liability or responsibility is incurred by the Appraiser in giving same." I immediately rushed to a jewelry store near Columbia and had it appraised again. The jeweler valued it at $350. I was relieved and pleased. That evening I wrote Laura a brief letter telling her to expect a small package in the mail. *When you get it, please don't open it until I call you,* I wrote. The following morning I mailed both the letter and the ring to Laura's new address.

She had moved into a one-bedroom apartment on 660 Main Street in Santa Clara, near the university. She had decided that it was more academically advantageous to get her Spanish teaching credential at the University of Santa Clara than at San Jose State. She shared the apartment with our friend Trudy McCulloch, who was studying for her high school teaching credential in math.

Five days later I anxiously called Laura from a phone booth in Hartley Hall, hoping that by now she had received my letter and surprise package. Trudy answered the phone. "I am glad you called," she said in her deep, raspy voice. "Laura's been on pins and needles since yesterday, wondering what's in the box you sent her. And frankly, I am, too . . . Here's Laura."

"Hi. It's so good to hear your voice," Laura said. "I miss you so much."

"I miss you, too," I said, feeling my throat tighten. "I hope you like what I got you."

"I'm dying to find out!"

I could hear and feel her excitement. "Open it," I responded, feeling proud of myself.

"I am opening it now," she said. There was a brief silence. "Oh my God!" she exclaimed. "It's beautiful! What a wonderful surprise!"

"I'm glad you like it," I said. "I'm sorry I wasn't able to give it to you before I left. I had to . . ."

"You don't need to explain," she said politely. "I understand . . . besides, it was worth the wait." Her tone was sweet and empathetic.

"Thank you," I said. "I feel very happy and peaceful inside."

"I do, too."

After we hung up, I went my room, thanked the Virgen de Guadalupe, and went to bed. I slept soundly that night.

Concentration

Before classes started, I was pleased to receive a notice from Professor Andrés Iduarte informing me that he was officially my academic advisor and inviting me to meet with him prior to registration to select courses and discuss topics for my master's thesis. I went to see him during his office hours on the third floor of Philosophy Hall. When I entered, he stood up from behind his desk, greeted me, and asked me to sit in a wooden chair next to him. His large, dark rectangular office had floor-to-ceiling bookshelves and an oval window opposite the entrance. Next to his wooden desk, which sat in the middle of the room facing the door, was a black three-drawer metal file cabinet. I thanked him for being my advisor, and we discussed and agreed on the classes I should take that year, including two of his classes for the fall semester: The Spanish American Essay and Directed Research. He picked up a pen from his neat desk, signed my course schedule, handed it to me, and said, "Now, have you thought about a topic for your thesis?"

"Something on Latin American literature, preferably Mexican," I responded.

"I am not surprised," he said. "But both are broad and rich fields from which to choose; you need to be specific."

"I guess I need more time to think about it," I responded after a brief moment of silence.

"That's fine," he said. "Choose a topic that excites you, something you feel passionate about."

I thanked him and agreed to meet with him again soon to finalize my choice.

I had ample material from which to pick. I had read works by many prominent Mexican and other Latin American writers the previous year and during the summer: Sor Juana Inés de la Cruz, considered one of the greatest Mexican poets of the seventeenth century; Mexican writers Mariano Azuela, Nellie Campobello, and Martín Luis Guzmán, whose novels chronicle the Mexican Revolution; Gabriela Mistral, a Chilean poet who received the Nobel Prize in Literature and had taught Spanish literature at Columbia; Miguel Ángel Asturias, a Guatemalan novelist and recipient of the Nobel Prize in Literature; the Argentine short story writer Jorge Luis Borges; and many others. In my readings I had discovered a preference for novels and short stories that depicted characters with whom I could identify: peasants, Indians, and mestizos. I was drawn to literary works that dealt with themes of social justice and reflected the reality of Mexico and Latin America.

After much reflection, I decided to write my thesis on the Indian in the novels of Gregorio López y Fuentes. I had written a paper the previous year on his classic novel *El Indio* for my course on the Mexican Revolution and had found similarities between Indian customs described in his work and my own family's way of life. In addition, I had picked strawberries in Santa Maria alongside *braceros*, a few of whom were Indians from rural parts in southern Mexico. I recalled that on my birth certificate, which I had to obtain after we got deported to Mexico when I was fourteen, I was classified as "*indígena*," indigenous—a term used by the Mexican census to report the cultural ethnicity of individuals.

I met with Professor Iduarte a second time and told him of my decision. He thought the topic an excellent choice and, to help me with my research, gave me Fernando Benítez's *Los indios de México*, The Indians of Mexico, and Frank Tannenbaum's *The Mexican Agrarian Revolution* and *Mexico: The Struggle for Peace and Bread*. He said that Benítez was the expert on Mexican Indian cultures and Tannenbaum was a well-known and respected historian on the Columbia faculty who had done research on rural education in Mexico for many years and had served as advisor to Mexican president Lázaro Cárdenas. Before I left his office, Professor Iduarte also asked that I give him an outline of my thesis before the end of the semester.

I began working on the outline, skimming various master's theses in Butler Library on both Spanish Peninsular and

Latin American authors to get an idea of what was expected. Every one of the essays contained an analysis of the author's life and works within a historical framework. Using them as a model, I wrote an outline and submitted it to Professor Iduarte. We discussed it the week before Thanksgiving break. "*Está muy bien hecho, Panchito.*" It's very well done, he said.

I teared up. In his tone I heard my father's voice—I missed him and the rest of my family so much.

He glanced out the window, then looked straight into my eyes and said, "I notice you get a little emotional sometimes when I call you Panchito and when we talk about Mexico . . ."

"I do," I said apologetically. I told him that my nickname connected me to my family and my childhood and that I felt a strong bond to Mexico, even though my family came to the United States when I was four years old. "*Es mi tierra natal, mi herencia cultural, pero también me siento ser americano.*" It's my native land, my cultural heritage, but I also feel that I am an American. I had become a naturalized American citizen only a few years earlier.

"*Es natural que te sientas ser de dos culturas; eres mexicano y americano.*" It's natural to feel that you are part of two cultures; you're Mexican and American, he said. "*Y tus antepasados?*" What about your ancestors?

I related to him that my paternal grandfather, Hilario, was a small farmer who died in 1910, when my father was a few months old; that my maternal grandfather, Salvador Hernández, was a mule driver who chopped and sold wood for a living; and that according to my Tía Chana, my grandmothers were both very religious, humble, honest, and hard working, as were my grandfathers.

"*Así es nuestro pueblo.*" That's how our people are, he said proudly. He got up from behind his desk, picked up a book from the shelf, and handed it to me. "This is Justo Sierra's *Evolución política del pueblo mexicano* [Political Evolution of the Mexican People]. It's for you to read and keep." I stood up and thanked him. Before I left his office, he gave me a hug and added, "*Mano a la obra, Panchito.*" Get to work.

I felt fortunate and excited about having Andrés Iduarte as my advisor and teacher and about what I was learning.

As I read Justo Sierra's history of Mexico and Gregorio López y Fuentes's novels, I became more troubled by the social, political, and economic injustices suffered by the Indians in Mexico since the Spanish conquest and more aware of the need to value and incorporate their culture into the nation's life and identity. López y Fuentes's work reminded me of John Steinbeck's *The Grapes of Wrath*, which I read in high school; it was the first literary work to which I could relate.

In the course of study for my master's I became interested in the issue of race in Latin America in the nineteenth century. As a result, I wrote the final paper for Andrés Iduarte's Spanish American Essay class on José Martí, a Cuban essayist, poet, and journalist who devoted his entire life to freeing Cuba from Spain and to establishing a democracy without slavery. Unlike most of his contemporaries, who claimed that

Indians and blacks were inferior to whites, Martí believed in the equality of all races. He wrote, "Anything that divides men from each other, that separates them, singles them out, or hems them in, is a sin against humanity." His ideas on race were universal and timeless.

José Martí and Gregorio López y Fuentes influenced my own thinking about social justice and my heritage. I respected them and other authors who used their writing talent to combat injustices in society.

Rebellion from Within

Things were falling into place my second year of graduate school. I had done well in my classes, had made good progress on my thesis, and looked forward to getting married in the summer. But my protected world at Columbia was being shaken. Rallies against the Vietnam War at the Sundial, demonstrations against class rank reporting, and confrontations with military recruiters dominated the campus. Anyone could feel the tension in the air.

The increasing protests on campus against the Vietnam War, a war that I opposed, were constant reminders of the possibility of my being drafted into the army. On February 16, 1968, the National Selective Service System eliminated deferments for nearly all graduate students except those going into ministry, medicine, dentistry and related health fields, and, fortunately for me, all students in their second year or beyond. I thought I was exempt from the draft as long as I remained studying full-time. But on February 19, 1968, I got a letter from my draft board informing me that I had been granted a deferment only until October of that year (local draft boards had discretion in granting exemptions on the basis of community and defense needs). I felt anxious and uncertain about the draft beyond that year even though I had been awarded a National Defense Foreign Language Fellowship for 1968–69. It was one of only two such fellowships given to students in Columbia's Graduate Spanish Department that year. My hope was that the board would continue to extend my deferment until I could at least finish graduate school.

If my father knew that I was against the Vietnam War and that I did not volunteer to join the army, he would have been disappointed. His heart filled with pride when I gave him a picture of me in an army uniform, taken when I was in mandatory ROTC for two years in college. "I am proud of you, *mijo*," he said. "You can make something of yourself in the army when you're poor." It was the only picture he took with him when he had his nervous breakdown and left our family to return to Mexico.

My sympathy for antiwar demonstrations on campus and at other colleges and universities increased when I received a letter from Roberto telling me that my high school classmate and friend Dickie Giovanacci had been killed in Vietnam and that my brother Trampita had been drafted into the army. Now my younger sibling Juan Manuel "Torito" would need to take over Trampita's janitorial job to help support my family. I was scared for Trampita and sad and mad that thousands of men were being asked to fight in a war they questioned. I prayed for them and everyone in Vietnam: men, women, and children.

In addition to the protests against the war and the draft, many Columbia students objected to the university's plan to construct a new gym in Morningside Park as a joint project with the city. The facility was to have access for residents of Harlem through a lower level—a so-called back door—and an upper-level entrance for the predominantly white university community. *The Columbia Spectator*, the student newspaper, reported that protesters interpreted the plan as segregationist and therefore discriminatory and that they were planning to demonstrate at the construction site.

On the second day of the demonstration I walked over to Morningside Park, which was a couple of blocks from John Jay Hall. A large number of protesters had gathered and were tearing down the tall chainlink fence surrounding the construction site, yelling repeatedly, "Gym Crow, no go." Within minutes the police arrived and forcefully pulled and shoved the demonstrators away from the fence. A few who resisted were handcuffed and hauled into police cars. Feeling nervous but curious, I joined a small group of spectators and followed the rest of the protesters as they left Morningside Park and marched back to the middle of campus. We gathered around the Sundial, which was used as a podium by demonstrators. A young man with a bullhorn in his hand stepped onto it and introduced himself as Mark Rudd, president of Columbia's chapter of Students for a Democratic Society. He had long, wavy sandy hair, a prominent jaw, and narrow eyes, and he wore blue jeans, boots, and a rumpled shirt open at the neck. The crowd grew to about four hundred people. I felt a mixture of good humor and apprehension as I listened to his passionate and dramatic speech. He spoke against the university's move to build the "Gym Crow," and he talked of "the immoral war in Vietnam" and of "ending racism and sexism," and he urged the audience to support "underprivileged groups" in their efforts to gain better jobs, housing, schools, and equal treatment. What he was saying rang true to me. At the end of his talk he made his way through the crowd, followed by four students at his side. As he passed by me, I stretched out my hand to shake his and said, "Thank you." He glanced at me, nodded, and kept on walking. He had a determined, intense look in his eyes.

Amid all this turmoil, Martin Luther King, Jr., was assassinated while leading a strike by garbage collectors in Memphis. The news of his death stunned me. I was heartbroken. I admired and respected deeply his lifelong courageous nonviolent fight against racial prejudice in our country and his dedication and commitment to social justice and human dignity.

Four days after Dr. King's death, the chaplain at Columbia invited the community to a memorial service in St. Paul's Chapel on the afternoon of April 9. I arrived early and took a seat next to a tall black man dressed in a dark suit. Within minutes the chapel filled with mourners of all colors, young and old. Midway through the somber eulogy delivered by Columbia's vice president, Mark Rudd got up from his aisle seat, walked slowly and deliberately to the front of the chapel, and cut in front of the vice president. He took over the pulpit, grabbed the microphone, and declared that the service was a moral outrage against the memory of Dr. King. He criticized the administration for eulogizing a man who had died while trying to unionize sanitation workers when the university had fought the unionization of its own black and Puerto Rican employees and had stolen land from the people of Harlem to build a gymnasium. Rudd said the tribute was an "obscenity," given Columbia's mistreatment of blacks and workers, whom King had championed and for whom he lost his life. Rudd left the pulpit, walked down the center aisle with shoulders slightly hunched forward, and exited the chapel, followed by several attendees. I was shocked. His rude behavior offended and disappointed me. The vice president finished his eulogy, ignoring what had happened. At the end of the tribute we all held hands and sang "Amazing Grace" and "We Shall Overcome." A wave of sadness came over me.

After that incident, tensions built as protesters led by Rudd seized five campus buildings, including the president's office, took a dean hostage for a short period of time, and broke doors, windows, and furniture.

Steve Winter and I had a discussion about the demonstrators during one of our sloppy joe dinners.

"I support students' efforts to end the war and racial bigotry and social injustices," I said to Steve, "but taking over buildings and disrespecting the rights of others . . . that's wrong."

"Rubbish, mate," he said. "If institutions don't listen to students and other oppressed people in your country, then they have to resort to aggressive action; it's their only alternative."

"If by 'aggressive action' you mean violence, I don't agree," I said. "I joined César Chávez on a march to Sacramento my senior year in college. It was a peaceful march of farm workers who demanded an end to being exploited in the fields. It was successful."

"Because it was peaceful?" he asked. I heard a tone of doubt in his voice.

"Of course!" I said emphatically. "But it was only one victory in a long struggle that continues to this day. I remember Chávez leading the march. Farm workers followed, carrying the American flag, the Mexican flag, the flag from the Philippines, and a large banner of the Virgen de Guadalupe. It was like a pilgrimage."

Our debate went on without us agreeing, but we were respectful of each other's point of view.

Unfortunately, after several days of negotiations between the administration and the protesters that failed to resolve the crisis, Columbia's president decided to call the police onto the campus. I, among a crowd of nearly a thousand students gathered at the Sundial, heard it announced by a university official in the early evening on Monday, April 29. Dressed neatly in a three-piece suit, the official stepped onto the Sundial and, raising the bullhorn to his mouth, his voice breaking, told us that the police would be arriving on campus shortly. He demanded that we go back to our dorms or leave via the nearest gate. Student protesters began shouting repeatedly, "It's our campus—cops must go!" I broke through the crowd and walked quickly back to my dorm, passing in front of Hamilton Hall, where a group of protesters shouted, "We shall not be moved; cops don't scare us, we shall not be moved." Some carried posters of Che Guevara and Malcolm X. At the same time, a detachment of twenty or so policemen gathered in front of John Jay Hall. I could feel my heart racing as a policeman blocked the entrance and did not let me through. "This is my dorm; I live here," I said. My mouth felt as dry as if I had been chewing a handkerchief. After I showed the officer my Columbia ID, he opened the glass door and shoved me inside with his nightstick. Shaking and confused, I rushed up to my room and watched from my window. Protesters who had taken over Hamilton Hall kept on shouting "No violence, no violence, police must go!" and "Up against the wall." After a long while I collapsed in bed, emotionally exhausted. The night seemed eerie. I dozed off and on, glancing at the clock each time I awoke. Suddenly, sirens pierced the morning silence. I jumped out of bed, frightened and groggy, and looked out the window. Hundreds of helmeted police officers had formed a line across the College Walk, trying to disburse a mass of students several rows deep. The protesters had locked arms and refused to move. Within minutes, several hundred more policemen joined the ranks and began to move forward with force. They smashed through the student barricade and began clubbing a few in the front row. The demonstrators resisted and then scrambled and fled. The police ran after them, swiping at their legs and heads with billy clubs.

I was terrified. I had witnessed police brutality only one other time in my life, when, as a child, I saw the Border Patrol raid Tent City. Several Border Patrol vans had come to a screeching halt one afternoon and blocked the entrance to the labor camp where my family and other farm laborers lived. The officers, dressed in green uniforms and armed, swept through the tents looking for undocumented workers, who ran into the wilderness behind the camp, trying to escape. The officers chased after them, and when the workers tripped and fell to the ground, the patrolmen struck them with their billy clubs, kicked them in the ribs, dragged them into the vans, and hauled them away.

I could not believe that the kind of violence I had witnessed in Tent City was taking place at Columbia University, which I thought of as a bastion of grandeur, knowledge, refinement, and civility. After the police had violently quashed the demonstration, it took me a long time to calm down. I was angry at the police brutality and disappointed and upset with the university administration for calling them onto the campus.

The next day *The New York Times* reported that the New York Police Department had ended the demonstration and forcefully removed protesters from occupied buildings. The campus "bust" resulted in forty-seven arrests and sixty-eight reported injuries. Classes were canceled for the rest of the week.

After that horrible and shocking night, I was more convinced than ever that social justice must be sought through peaceful means.

So Far yet So Close

By the middle of spring, campus life returned to normal. Classes resumed after being canceled for a week during the riots, which resulted in the suspension of twenty student protesters, including Mark Rudd, and the cancellation of the plans to construct the gym. Political demonstrations were now confined to the Sundial area. In a few days, after finals, I would be going home for the summer. I could hardly contain my excitement to see Laura and my family again and to get married.

What kept me going during those long and lonely months were the letters I received from my mother, Roberto and Darlene, and Laura; the expected visit from Laura during the Christmas holidays; and occasional phone calls.

Unfortunately, my hope for spending time with her that Christmas, which I had anticipated like a child, vanished when she canceled her trip a few days before she was to come to New York. I had arranged with Columbia's housing office for her to stay in a guest room in a women's residence hall.

Laura wrote a letter telling me that her maternal grandparents, who took care of her and her sister after Laura's mother died, had told her that it was not proper for her to visit me, as we were not yet married. They were concerned about what people might think: How could Laura and Francisco spend the holidays together without supervision? I was crushed, but I understood her grandparents' reasoning. My parents would have done the same thing. They were very protective of my sister and did not allow her to date, even though she was a teenager. My father was less strict with us boys. He allowed my older brother and me to go out once a week when we were in our late teens, as long as we abided by his midnight curfew. I called Laura that evening after reading her letter. She was upset and painfully apologetic.

"I am so sorry," she said. Her voice cracked.

"No need to apologize. I understand perfectly," I said. "Of course I am as disappointed as you are, but we have to obey them even if we disagree with them, out of respect."

"I knew you'd understand," Laura said. "I feel the same way; that's why I didn't argue with them. My grandparents said you'd be terribly angry with them . . . that you would try to convince me to come visit you anyway. They'll be surprised when I tell them your reaction, but they'll be pleased."

After our call, I wrote Laura a brief note: *Our hearts are one; they pain us in their suffering to come together.*

Just as it was last year, the dorm was like a tomb on Christmas Day, but I felt less lonely this time. I went to Mass and to the movies to see *In the Heat of the Night*. I spent the rest of the Christmas break working on my thesis and preparing for finals.

Laura and I wrote to each other at least once a week, and every time I received a letter from her it was like getting a Christmas present. We wrote about our college days, when we studied and worked together in the language lab, took walks around the Mission Gardens, and played the nickel pinball machine at a smoke shop near the university. We also shared ideas about having children and raising them to be kind, loving, generous, compassionate, and respectful, and about providing them with a good, stable home and a good education. Laura wrote about her classes for her teaching credential and the challenges and joys of student teaching, and about going with Wanda to look for a wedding dress. I mailed her information about teaching positions in New York City. She sent me pictures of different silverware patterns and asked me to help her choose one. *Whatever you pick is fine with me*, I wrote. *Growing up, we used tortillas for silverware.*

Besides our weekly letters, Laura and I talked on the phone at least twice a month in the beginning but, thanks to the kindness of a telephone operator, more often as time passed.

I always called Laura from the same phone booth in Hartley Hall in the late evenings, when the rates went down. I would dial for operator assistance and deposit a dollar and a quarter in change for the first three minutes. I tried to limit our conversations to that amount of time. However, I lost track of time on one occasion when Laura and I were talking about whom we should invite to our wedding. The operator interrupted us in the middle of our conversation and said that I had fifteen seconds left and I needed to deposit another dollar and a quarter for the next three minutes if I wished to continue. I told her I did not have any more change. She must have heard the frustration in my voice because she offered to bill me for the rest of the call beyond the three minutes. I thanked her and gave her my name and address so she could send me the bill. Days later, I called Laura again. I paid for the initial three minutes, ran overtime, and asked the operator to bill me for the remainder of the call. To my surprise, I never got a bill for either of the two calls nor for the overtime calls I made after that. I had no idea who the operator was, but each time I called, she greeted me and asked me how I was doing. One time I placed a call to Laura's parents' phone because she had gone home for the weekend. After I dialed, the operator came on and said, "This isn't the number you've been calling. I hope you're not calling a different girl."

"I'm calling my fiancée at her parents' home," I responded, laughing.

"Just checking," she said. "Please deposit a dollar and a quarter for the first three minutes."

I smiled to myself and thanked her.

Underlying our letters and phone conversations was the frustration we both felt about not being able to put into words what we felt for each other.

You make me feel like April after the rain—or the sunshine at 7:00 in the morning, Laura wrote. . . . *the closer the end of the year gets, the more impatient I become for the day when words will no longer be necessary.*

I, too, longed for that day. It was soon to come.

"Today I Am Born"

I could feel the excitement down to the tips of my fingers as I grabbed my ticket for the TWA flight to San Francisco at Columbia Travel Service on West 113th Street. I was going home for the summer to visit my family and marry Laura.

It was Wednesday, May 15, seven days before finals week and nine days before the flight. I turned the final research papers in to my professors on Thursday, May 23, and got ready to leave the following day. On Thursday, Steve Winter and I had our last sloppy joe supper and took the elevator down to the Lion's Den for a beer, which reminded me of Phillip Andrews's farewell a year and a half earlier. However, Steve was not leaving. He had rented a one-bedroom apartment in the basement of a commercial building on the East Side and planned to start his own architecture business from there. He offered Laura and me a sublet of his place for the month of September for sixty-seven dollars while we looked for a place of our own after our wedding. He was going to London to visit his sister. To thank him, I gave him my cooking gear but told him I could not reveal my recipe for sloppy joes. In return, he allowed me to store my stuff in his place, which looked like a long, narrow dungeon.

On Friday morning I packed my small brown suitcase, which was given to me when I graduated from high school by the Madrinas Club, a charitable Latina organization in Santa Maria. I placed my unfinished master's thesis in a vinyl zipped bag and, for safekeeping, tucked it between my clothes. Then I turned in my room key at the main desk in Hartley Hall and headed out to Kennedy Airport.

During the six-hour flight I gazed periodically out the window at the white, fluffy clouds floating by and the sun rays guiding the plane to San Francisco. The thought of Laura sitting next to me on my way back to Columbia after our wedding in August made me smile.

From the San Francisco airport I took a bus to Redwood City and switched to another bus to San Jose, which made local stops along the way. I finally arrived at Santa Clara after spending two and a half hours on the road. It was eight p.m. Weary but excited, I hurried impatiently on foot to the apartment complex at 660 Main Street and rushed up the stairs to the second floor, unit number four. My heart was racing. I set my suitcase down, wiped the sweat off my forehead with my shirtsleeve, and knocked on the door.

Laura answered. "Oh my God, you're really here!" she exclaimed. "It's been so long!"

Seeing Laura again felt like a dream. Our eyes watered and, trembling with excitement, we embraced and kissed. Trudy, Laura's roommate, came out of her room and gave me a warm hug. After we calmed down, Laura stretched out her hand and proudly showed me her engagement ring. On her hand it looked more strikingly beautiful than I had imagined.

She gave me the good news that she had accepted a job in New York, teaching Spanish beginning that fall at Notre Dame Academy High School, a college preparatory Catholic school for girls run by the Sisters of the Congregation of Notre Dame. We looked up Staten Island on a map and decided to search for a place to live near the school, once we got to New York City.

"Your commute to Columbia shouldn't be too bad," Laura said.

"I don't think so," I responded, not giving it much thought. "Things are falling into place, thank God."

We stayed up late, catching up and going over details for our wedding party: the Reverend Father John B. Shanks, S.J., my spiritual advisor and mentor in college, would perform the wedding ceremony; Lynn would be maid of honor; the bridesmaids were Marsha and Betty Beetley, Laura's best friend and roommate in college; Roberto would be best man and Torito and Ron Whitcanack ushers. Ron was my college friend and character witness when I became an American citizen. We also talked about how wonderful it would be if my father could attend our wedding. We sent him an invitation and told him that our whole family was eager to see him and that all of us had agreed to pay for his travel.

I spent that night and the night after in Randy Chun's apartment, which was on the first floor of the apartment complex. (Randy was a mutual friend from our college days at the University of Santa Clara.) The next day, Saturday, we took a long walk and went over the list of people we had invited to our wedding.

Early Sunday morning Laura's father and her uncle Alfred, a tall, handsome, athletically built man, came by to see Laura and me and to help her pack some of her belongings. She was moving out of the apartment in the middle of June to live with her parents during the summer to prepare for the wedding.

Oreste was friendly but distant. He and Alfred sat across the kitchen table from Laura and me and laughed and joked together. They reminisced about the time they both played baseball. Oreste was an all-star player in high school and junior college. Alfred played professional ball for the Boston Braves but was drafted into the army at the height of his career to fight in the Korean War. When I asked him about his participation in the war, he lowered his voice and grabbed a paper napkin from the chrome dispenser. Rolling it tightly with his agile fingers, he said, "I'd rather not talk about it."

"It was a painful experience," Oreste said, putting his arm around his brother's broad shoulders. "Let's get going." He pushed the chair back and stood up, both legs slightly apart, as though ready for a baseball to be hit his way.

After we finished loading the boxes into Oreste's four-door black Plymouth, he offered to drop me off at the Greyhound bus station in downtown San Jose. I was on my way home to Santa Maria, where I had a job interview on Monday for a position as coordinator of the Economic Opportunity Commission for Santa Barbara County. Laura and I tearfully said goodbye. To have to be apart again so soon was sad for both of us, but knowing that we would be getting married in a few weeks was consoling.

When I arrived in Santa Maria, Roberto picked me up at the run-down bus station on Broadway. As soon as I saw him, I felt a wave of happiness, warmth, and nostalgia. I would be spending my last summer at home with him and his family. They had more living space in their three-bedroom tract home than my mother had in her modest two-bedroom house, where she and three of my younger siblings lived.

Late that afternoon Roberto and Darlene had a barbecue in their backyard and invited our whole family and friends to welcome me. It was a joyful occasion, but I missed Laura and wished Trampita and my father had been there too.

Monday morning I had my interview with the Santa Barbara County Education Office and was told that even though I qualified for the position, they were not willing to invest in my training for only a summer position. They preferred to hire someone permanently. I was terribly disappointed but not discouraged. I immediately contacted the Southern Counties Gas Company of California, and fortunately, they had an opening in the office, tracking, recording, and filing industrial gas meter usage and operations. I began work the following Monday, June 3. The job was tedious and routine, but it required focus and accuracy, which distracted me from worrying about school and daydreaming about Laura.

For the next few weeks Laura and I kept in touch mostly through phone calls and letters, and on two occasions I borrowed Roberto's car and drove up to San Carlos on the weekend. Another time she came down by bus to spend a weekend with my family and me. We shopped together in downtown Santa Maria for her wedding ring and bought one for $13.13 at Melby's Jewelers on West Main Street. The store was owned by George Herikami, for whom my father, Roberto, and I had worked picking strawberries from time to time when George was a sharecropper.

At times it seemed as though nothing had changed—Laura and I were still apart. Every day when I returned home from work I would ask Darlene the same question: "Did I get any mail?" She often answered before I had a chance to ask. We both laughed whenever this happened.

Then one day I received a letter with bad news: my father was not coming to our wedding. He wrote:

. . . *Siento mucho no poder ir a tu boda, Panchito. Dios no me dio licencia de poder ir. Me siento muy enfermo, con dolores de*

estómago, y he estado muy nervioso y con miedo, pero Dios dirá.
Felicitaciones, Panchito y Laurita. Según me dices, Panchito, Lau-
rita es un tesoro y debes cuidarla mucho y también tu nuevo hogar
porque un hogar bueno es lo mejor del mundo. Me siento tan feliz
que todos ustedes no me olviden porque lo único que tengo en este
mundo es a ustedes. . . . Me tiré al sufrimiento en Los Estados
Unidos por estar todos juntos hasta que pude pero mi cuerpo me
falló. Que Dios me los cuide y proteja. Les mando muchos abrazos
y nunca los olvidaré. . . . I am very sorry I can't go to your
wedding, Panchito. It was not God's will. I feel very sick with
stomach pains, and have been very nervous and fearful, but
it's up to God. Congratulations, Panchito and Laurita. According to what you tell me, Panchito, Laurita is a treasure,
and you should take good care of her and your new home
because a good home is what's best in this world. I feel so
happy that all of you have not forgotten me, because the only
thing I have in this world is you. I threw myself into suffering
in the United States to have us all together as long as I could,
but my poor body failed me. May God take care of you and
protect you. I send you many hugs and will never forget you.

Laura and I were deeply disappointed that he could not
be at our wedding, and heartbroken that he continued to suffer from illness. When I shared the letter with the rest of my
family, they were heartbroken too. We wrote him to tell him
that we loved and missed him and urged him to see a doctor
instead of relying on a *curandera*. Our hope that he would get

well and return to us was fading, but my mother held on to her dream that he would eventually come back. Deep inside I wanted to believe that her dream would come true.

On weekends I helped Roberto clean a few business offices, which he had as side jobs. After work we would often visit our mother and younger brothers Torito and Ruben and younger sister, Rorra, and then go to a Pizza Hut for a beer and talk about our childhood and family. Roberto was like a second father to my siblings and me, and Darlene was like our big sister. One Saturday I baby-sat for their three little girls—Jackie, Angela, and Laura. *The babies are so good,* I wrote Laura, *I can hardly wait til we have our own. The lovely relationship that Roberto and Darlene have makes me more anxious for August 17 to come.*

On Friday morning, the day before our wedding day, my family and I drove to San Carlos, checked in at the Travelodge, which was off the El Camino, near the Villa Hotel, where the rehearsal dinner was to take place. We changed our clothes and headed to Saint Charles Church for the wedding rehearsal. Father Shanks was waiting for us at the entrance to the church. He greeted everyone and gave each of us directions rapidly and energetically about what to say and do during the ceremony.

After the rehearsal we drove to the Villa Hotel. Mrs. Marian Hancock, whose late husband was a wealthy industrialist and philanthropist in Santa Maria, hosted the dinner. She had learned of my family's financial situation when I worked for her one year delivering Christmas presents; and when she received our wedding invitation, she graciously offered to host the dinner. Margie Williams, her personal secretary, made all the arrangements. Included at the dinner, besides the wedding party, were Margie Williams and her husband; Laura's maternal grandparents, Caterina and Rico; her paternal grandmother, Rosa; my younger siblings; and Marie and Tollie Golmon, Mrs. Hancock's close friends for whom I worked the summer Laura and I got engaged. My family and I were overwhelmed by Mrs. Hancock's generosity.

That night I had a hard time falling asleep. It seemed impossible that the day I so eagerly had waited for was only a few hours away. But I also felt nervous. I was about to make a commitment for the rest of my life. *I hope I can be as good a husband as Roberto*, I thought.

Early the next morning, on our way to Saint Charles Church, I confessed my worries and anxieties to Roberto. "These feelings are normal," he assured me. "Everything will be okay, Panchito."

We got to the church by ten thirty and were surprised to see that many family members and friends had already arrived. I felt uncomfortable wearing a morning suit and getting so much attention.

The wedding ceremony began at eleven with organ music and the processional. At the end of the procession Laura came up the aisle escorted by her father. Looking like an angel in a gorgeous full-length white dress with short lace sleeves, a short veil, and a train attached to the back, she carried a bouquet of small white roses. As they approached the altar, I stepped forward and faced them. Oreste gave Laura's hand to me and grinned. He stepped back and joined Wanda in the first pew. Both of them had watery eyes. Laura and I smiled at each other and squeezed hands. Her large brown eyes sparkled like stars. Father Shanks greeted Laura and me and then the guests. He explained that our wedding rite, the sacrament of matrimony, was one of the seven sacraments of God's grace. We all joined in an opening prayer, and after the Bible readings, Father Shanks gave a moving homily on the meaning of marriage. Laura and I then exchanged vows and rings. Inside of mine Laura had inscribed *"Hoy he nacido,"* Today I am born. It was the title and first line of a poem by Amado Nervo, a nineteenth-century Mexican poet. At that moment, my heart pounded with joy. She and I were now one in marriage for the rest of our lives.

At the conclusion of the wedding she and I walked together down the aisle, surrounded by friends and family, ready to start our new life.

At the reception at the Elks Lodge in San Mateo, Roberto handed me a telegram from Steve Winter. It read, *Mexican worm finally emerges from cocoon to become butterfly and fly away with beautiful Italian flower. Good luck.*

Making a Home

A week after spending an enjoyable and memorable three-day honeymoon in Lake Tahoe under cloudy and rainy skies, Laura and I took a redeye flight from San Francisco to New York City, arriving bleary-eyed at Kennedy Airport at six thirty in the morning. It was the Thursday before Labor Day weekend. We picked up our luggage, hailed a cab, and headed to Greenwich Village. The air was hot and muggy.

Steve Winter, who promised to rent us his apartment for the month of September while he visited his sister in London, had to cancel his plans and remain in New York until the end of the month and then move to Connecticut to begin working for an architectural firm. He made arrangements for us to stay at his friend's apartment in Greenwich Village as house sitters for a few days while they went on a short vacation. He gave us the address and told us to pick up the key from the super, the manager of the apartment complex.

Laura and I felt uncomfortable and nervous about staying in a strange place whose owners we had not met.

The apartment was on the first floor of a four-story red-brick building. It had one bedroom, a small, cluttered living room, and a narrow kitchen with a stained dirty sink and a large cabinet above it containing stacked multicolor dishes and worn-out pots and pans. There were potted plants throughout the place, giving it a damp and musty odor. Two fat black cats gingerly wandered around the apartment, poking their heads from behind the furniture, as though spying on us. Cockroaches scurried away and hid when we turned on the lights. They reminded me of the hundreds of fleas that invaded our beds at night when my family lived in the army barrack in Bonetti Ranch. The tiny creatures fed on skinny stray dogs that roamed the migrant camp during the day and took refuge under our dwelling when the sun went down.

Laura's eyes got bigger with every cockroach that crossed her path.

Even though we were weary, we cleaned the apartment after we unpacked. She scoured the kitchen sink, wiped food crumbs from the dining table, and scrubbed the grimy toilet and moldy shower. Making good use of my janitorial experience, I dusted furniture and swept and mopped the filthy floors. When we finished, I thanked Laura and told her that my father would be proud of us.

"Why?" she asked, frowning and wiping her forehead with her sleeve.

"Because he insisted that we leave places we lived in

cleaner than we found them. It was a way of thanking the owner and increasing our chances of being welcomed if we ever came back."

Laura smiled. "Your dad is very wise."

Thursday evening we had dinner at Steve Winter's apartment. He was happy to meet Laura and to treat us to a homemade meal—Hungarian dumpling stew. He said it was a favorite recipe passed on to his family by his Hungarian maternal grandparents, who had immigrated to Australia many years ago. Laura talked about the long tradition in her family of making ravioli right after Thanksgiving in preparation for Christmas dinner every year, and I bragged about my mother's delicious *carne de puerco con chile colorado*, pork meat in red chili sauce and handmade flour tortillas. We each argued that our own family's dish was the best.

Friday morning we bought the New York *Daily News* and looked through ads for apartment rentals in Staten Island, hoping to find a place near Laura's school. Among the few listings was a rental agency. I called it first, thinking it would save us a lot of time and effort. "We do have only one apartment available; it's in a good location," the agent said. "Could I please have your name?"

"Francisco and Laura Jiménez," I responded excitedly.

I spelled out our last name for him and explained that the letter *j* in Spanish had the sound of the letter *h* in English. I had gotten into the habit of doing this to avoid the misspelling of it.

There was dead silence. Then he said, "I am terribly sorry. I made a mistake. The apartment has been rented."

My heart fell to my stomach. After I hung up, I wondered if the agent had told me the truth. Were we experiencing the sort of discrimination my friend Aldo Nelson and I had at the coffee shop in Paso Robles when the waitress refused to serve him because he was black?

I went down the list and called a few more places and got the same discouraging results: the apartments were no longer available or were too expensive.

Feeling anxious, Laura and I decided to rent a car and drive to Staten Island to look at the apartments remaining on our list. Notre Dame High School would be our starting point. We got a Ford sedan at a seedy Rent-A-Wreck place in lower Manhattan, and using a map of New York, Laura gave me driving directions. Once we crossed the Verrazano-Narrows Bridge and entered Staten Island, we were pleasantly surprised and happy to see so much greenery and open space. "Did you ever think that by marrying me you'd be living on an island?" I said.

"We haven't found a place to live yet," she said, laughing. "Keep your eyes on the road."

We ascended slowly up a grade for about two miles until we arrived at Notre Dame Academy High School. Overlooking a large lake and golf course, the school sat on several acres of lush green lawns, shrubs, and pine and cypress trees. It was a Colonial-style mansion—a huge two-story white rectangular structure with a panel front door framed by two pillars, large windows on the ground level, and slightly smaller ones on the second level. "What a beautiful setting for a school," Laura said. "And the view is spectacular. You can see the Verrazano-Narrows Bridge and the Manhattan skyline from here!"

"It feels like we're on top of the world," I said.

We left the school and went back down the hill, turned onto Victory Boulevard, a major thoroughfare on Staten Island, and began our long, frustrating search. The few rentals available were beyond our budget or inadequate—such as a one-room unit with no kitchen and a postage-size bathroom. By the middle of the afternoon Laura and I were tired and extremely anxious. I had the same feeling I had as a child when my family followed seasonal crops. Every time we moved, we worried about not finding a place to live.

Exhausted and disappointed, we decided to return to Greenwich Village. On our way back on Victory Boulevard we spotted a large sign advertising Grymes Hill Apartments. "Let's take a chance and see if they have anything available," Laura said wearily.

I glanced at my watch. It was close to five o'clock. "It's too late," I said. "The office will be closed. It's a three-day weekend."

Laura insisted. I could hear and feel her desperation. We turned onto Howard Avenue and followed the signs to a huge red-brick apartment complex, which turned out to be less than a mile from Victory Boulevard. We parked the car, rushed to the office, and asked a middle-aged woman, who was the office manager, if she had any rentals available.

"I am sorry," she said. "We have no vacancies."

Laura glanced at me with tears in her eyes. "Nothing at all?" she said. "Nothing . . ." Her voice cracked and slowly faded, like a wounded dove, and she burst into tears.

I put my arm around her shoulders and whispered, "We'll find something. Don't worry."

The woman must have taken pity on us. "Well . . . there's one possibility. A man reserved a studio apartment and we are holding it for him. If we don't hear from him by Tuesday morning, you can have it."

"That would be wonderful," Laura said, sighing and wiping her tears with the back of her hand.

"It's quite small and unfurnished. It's three hundred and ten square feet, but it's only a hundred and thirty dollars a month," the office manager said.

The monthly rent was more than we had expected to pay. Laura and her roommate had paid ninety dollars a month for an ample one-bedroom apartment in Santa Clara.

"We'll take anything, even if it's a closet," Laura said.

We all laughed.

"How far is Notre Dame Academy High School from here?" I asked. "We won't have a car."

"It's really close—about a mile, a twenty-minute walk," she said.

Laura and I looked at each other gleefully.

"Give me call on Tuesday morning," she said, handing me her business card and walking us out the door.

We thanked her repeatedly.

On Tuesday morning we nervously called the Grymes Hill Apartments business office and got the news: the studio apartment was available! They asked us to come to the office to sign a lease. We took the Seventh Avenue subway to the South Ferry Terminal at the southernmost tip of Manhattan and boarded the double-decker ferry to Staten Island. At a distance, we saw the Statue of Liberty and Ellis Island. Laura became emotional as she described how Ellis Island was the entry point for her paternal grandfather, Ferdinando Facchini, who left Italy for the United States when he was in his early twenties. A half-hour later we disembarked at the St. George Ferry Terminal, took a bus up Victory Boulevard, and got off at the Arlo Road stop. From there we walked up Howard Avenue for about a quarter of a mile to the Grymes Hill Apartments. As we approached the office, I said to Laura, "This is the route I'll be taking when I commute to Columbia."

"It's a lot of traveling back and forth. I am sorry," she said.

"Don't worry. I won't be going to Columbia every day—maybe three or four times a week. Besides, living here will be a refuge from the busy and noisy city."

Sight unseen, we signed the lease on the apartment and

paid the first and last month's rent. Our address was 520 Howard Avenue, apartment 1-A. Although small, the apartment was nice and clean. The front door was black, and the rectangular living room and bedroom combination had a light-color hardwood floor, a large front window with white venetian blinds and a steam heater underneath it, a kitchenette with a gas range and half-size refrigerator, and a small bathroom with a shower over the bathtub.

Happy and tired, we returned the rental car and spent another night at the apartment in Greenwich Village.

Early the next morning we took the subway up to Columbia so that Laura could see it and to look for notices on bulletin boards listing used furniture for sale. I gave her a quick tour, showing her John Jay Hall, the Lion's Den, and the phone booth in Hartley Hall from where I had made all the calls to her. We found a flyer listing several pieces of household items for sale at an apartment near the university. The owner, who was refurnishing her apartment, gave us a good deal on a sofa bed, two wooden chairs, a set of nesting tables, and a table lamp.

Late that afternoon we rented a beat-up van from Rent-A-Wreck and called Steve Winter to meet us at the apartment where we were to pick up the furniture. Laura sat in the passenger's seat next to me as I drove up Broadway, gripping the steering wheel with both hands and silently praying for our safety. The van moved sluggishly along, making rattling noises, as if it were going to break into pieces at any moment.

Impatient drivers swerved past us, leaning on their horns and shaking their fists. I fixed my eyes ahead and tried to roll up the window to block the irritating sounds, but it was broken and closed only halfway. Every time I stepped on the brake to avoid hitting a car or prevent being hit by one, Laura dug her fingers into my leg and pushed her foot against the floor. We were shaking by the time we arrived. Steve was already there, waiting for us in front of the apartment building.

We loaded the furniture onto the van, and the three of us squeezed into the front seat and headed to Staten Island. Our drive there was just as daunting as I maneuvered my way defensively through congested traffic and impatient drivers. On the way, we stopped to pick up the things I had stored in Steve's place over the summer and to get our luggage in Greenwich Village.

After we finished unloading the furniture into our Grymes Hill apartment, we thanked Steve for his help, promised him a homemade dinner, and drove him to the ferry terminal to return home.

Laura and I were exhausted but happy. We slept in our own place for the first time.

The next day, we took advantage of having the van, drove to the Volunteers of America, a secondhand store in Staten Island, and bought a couple of pots and pans and dishes and the rest of the furniture we needed: a small dining table and two chairs, a three-drawer dresser, and an open-front class-room desk with metal legs. A five-by-four yellow area rug, with fringes round its borders, caught our eye. We wanted to get it, but the price of twenty dollars seemed too expensive. After loading the furniture into the van and pacing back and forth in front of the store, agonizing about whether or not to buy the rug, we went ahead and purchased it.

To match the color of the rug, we bought two pints of paint and I painted the dining table and chairs and dresser bright yellow. I was about to paint the heater with the leftover paint, but Laura politely asked me not to. I told her how my father would paint the kitchen walls in our army barrack with discarded paint we found in the city dump, and if he had any paint left over, he would apply it to anything in sight until it was all gone, because he hated waste. Laura smiled and said, "I admire your dad's thriftiness, but . . ."

"I know," I said, interrupting her and laughing. "It's too much yellow."

We placed the desk in the front right-hand corner of the apartment and, next to it, the army trunk, which served as a bookshelf. Above the desk we taped a colorful map of the world and the wallet-size picture of the Virgen de Guadalupe. We set the sofa bed up against the middle of the right wall, the dining table to the left of the sofa, and the chest of drawers across from it.

Before returning the van, we bought groceries and everyday cleaning supplies. I was amazed at how much things cost and how much we had spent. Our combined savings of eighteen hundred dollars was quickly disappearing. Fortunately, I would be getting my National Defense Foreign Language Fellowship stipend at the end of the month, when fall semester classes at Columbia began, and Laura would soon start her teaching job. I felt lucky and grateful. Laura and I were creating our own home.

Life on Grymes Hill

It was early in the morning on Monday, a week after Labor Day. Laura and I walked the scenic mile up Grymes Hill, past Wagner College, to Notre Dame Academy High School, where she was to spend the day at an orientation, attending meetings in preparation for the beginning of the new school year. She was visibly nervous but eager to start her first teaching job.

We were met at the front of the school by Sister Louise Finn, the principal, who gave us a brief tour of the fifteen-room building and introduced us to some of the faculty, who were in the teacher's lounge having coffee and chatting. All of them were in their early twenties or thirties and very friendly. The only thing that distinguished the nuns from the lay faculty was their dress. They wore calf-length gray skirts topped with white blouses and gray vests. Around their necks they wore simple silver crosses that hung from a black cord. And each wore a short gray veil outlined by a narrow white stripe.

Sister Finn was a few years older than the rest of the faculty, and unlike the other nuns, she wore a simple silver ring on her left hand, which, according to Laura, meant that she had taken final vows. Her demeanor was cordial but reserved. After the introductions, she turned to me and said, "I know that Laura graduated from the University of Santa Clara. What about you?" She appeared genuinely interested.

"I did too," I said. "That's where Laura and I met."

She moved her head slightly up and down in approval and smiled. "A fine Jesuit school," she said. "Like the Jesuits, we Notre Dame Sisters also focus on education and social justice. We believe education has the power to transform the world."

"I agree. That's why I decided to become a teacher."

She smiled again, lightly touching her silver crucifix with her left hand. "Laura and I must get to our first meeting," she said. "It was a pleasure meeting you. I am sure we'll be seeing you often." She turned to Laura and added, "We're happy you have joined us."

"Thank you, Sister."

Up until that point I had had little contact with nuns. Laura, on the other hand, had spent her four years of high school studying under the Sisters of Notre Dame in Belmont, California. She admired their preparation, teaching, and progressive religious views.

I said goodbye and headed to Columbia to meet with Professor Iduarte. It was half past nine. I walked quickly down Grymes Hill to Victory Boulevard and took a slow-moving city bus to the ferry terminal. After a half-hour boat ride to lower Manhattan, I boarded a crowded, stuffy subway train for the trip up to the university, arriving just in time for my eleven o'clock meeting with the professor. As I entered the main gate to campus and saw John Jay Hall towering in the distance, I recalled the two long and lonely years I had spent living there. A cold chill went up my spine.

I climbed the worn gray marble stairs to the third floor in Philosophy Hall to Professor Iduarte's office. He greeted me, shaking my hand, and motioned for me to take a seat next to his. He said he had just returned from Mexico City after traveling most of the summer in Europe, which explained why he looked fatigued. He had dark circles under his eyes, and his voice was raspier than usual. *"¿Qué hay de nuevo?"* What's new? he asked. When I told him about my getting married over the summer, he sprang out of his chair and gave me a hug. *"Felicidades, Panchito!"* He became increasingly interested and enthusiastic the more I talked about Laura and her family. *"Tengo ansias de conocerela."* I am anxious to meet her. I was touched and pleasantly surprised by his reaction, and I promised to bring Laura to meet him soon.

We discussed my thesis and the course work for the year. He told me that the expectation was for me to take the M.A. oral and written exams and finish the thesis by end of spring semester. I told him I was making good progress on it, promised I would be ready, and showed him a list of the classes I proposed to take that year to complete the course work for the Ph.D. Among them were The Generation of 1898 and Modernism, with Jack Himelblau, a visiting professor from Harvard; Nineteenth-Century Spanish American Poetry, with Eugenio Florit, a well-known Cuban poet who recited poetry by memory and did dramatic readings in class; and Libro de Buen Amor, with Gonzalo Sobejano, a specialist in contemporary Spanish Peninsular literature who had the reputation of giving meticulously organized, concise, and thought-provoking lectures. Professor Iduarte approved my choices and suggested that it would be advantageous to enroll in at least one course with every professor in the department and become familiar with their published works before taking my oral and written exams. I agreed and thanked him for his advice and added to my list History of the Spanish Language with Professor Frederick Jungemann.

After meeting with Professor Iduarte, I walked over to Butler Library to work on my thesis. On the side entrance, taped to the glass door, was a job announcement for an instructor to teach a Spanish conversation course in a pilot program for nurses at St. Luke's Hospital School of Nursing. The pay was ten dollars per hour, the highest hourly wage I had ever received, more than I had expected. *My parents could use this extra money*, I thought. The previous year, I had met a student nurse at the Lion's Den who mentioned that she had difficulty communicating with some patients, mainly Puerto Ricans and Dominicans, who spoke only Spanish. She was surprised and troubled when I told her that my father, who only spoke Spanish, felt frustrated and embarrassed when he couldn't understand or explain himself to the doctor and nurses at the hospital where he was being treated after he accidentally cut off his finger with a power saw. I jotted down the information from the announcement and rushed to St. Luke's Hospital, on the corner of 114th Street and Amsterdam Avenue, near Columbia. I entered the lobby and told the receptionist that I wished to speak with the director of the program. She politely asked me to have a seat. After I waited impatiently for a long time, the director finally came out, introduced herself, and invited me into her office for an interview. At the end of it, she offered me the job, teaching a two-hour class in the evenings on Mondays and Wednesdays.

When I arrived home that evening, I found Laura exhausted and worried about her teaching schedule, which consisted of five different classes and preparations: Spanish I, II, III, IV, and Advanced Placement Spanish Literature. The total number of students was more than a hundred. I offered to take over the AP class to lighten her workload, but she refused. "You have far too much to do already," she said sympathetically. I argued and finally convinced her by telling her that I wanted and needed teaching experience for future employment opportunities. When I told her about the job I had accepted at St. Luke's and my plan to send the earnings to my family, she fully agreed but emphasized her concern for my taking on too much work.

"I'll be okay," I said.

She gave me a skeptical look and said, "I worry about you, you know."

"I know," I said. "I worry about you, too. You're far away from your family for the first time in your life and starting a new job, teaching four different courses with over a hundred students. That's really hard work!"

"We'll just have to take care of each other," she said. "That's a joy, not work."

The next day, when we asked Sister Finn for her approval of my taking over the AP Spanish course for Laura and told her that we did not expect any additional compensation, she said, "Wonderful. Two for one is truly a gift from God." Unfortunately, the class had only eight students, which did little to reduce the overall enrollment in Laura's four classes.

My AP Spanish Literature class met at eight o'clock in the morning, Monday through Friday, in a small room with windows on two sides, overlooking the school gardens. The bright and eager seniors and I sat around a seminar table and discussed, in Spanish, literary pieces contained in an anthology. I related the readings to students' lives whenever possible and supplemented the textbook with *San Manuel Bueno, Mártir*, a novelette by Miguel de Unamuno in which the author explores the meaning of life and death and the struggle between faith and reason. I realized early on that I needed to learn more about how to present material interestingly and how to challenge students to think critically.

Because of our busy and hectic schedule during the week,

Laura and I saw each other only briefly: early mornings at six, when we got ready for work; during the twenty-minute walk to Notre Dame High School; and late evenings, often at eleven o'clock, when I got home after my last class at Columbia, which ended at seven, and doing research in the library. On weekends Laura did the laundry and we both took the bus to go grocery shopping at the A&P market. The task of carrying the grocery bags on the bus and hauling them up the hill to our apartment became more challenging when it rained or snowed. On Sundays, after Mass, Laura prepared lesson plans for the week, made up exams, or corrected papers. I reviewed material for my AP class, did research for my graduate courses, and worked on my thesis.

The Christmas holidays brought relief from our busy schedule, but not from the freezing weather on Grymes Hill. We tacked the yellow rug to the inside of the front door to shield us from icy winds that sliced through the narrow gaps around the door frame. We put on flannel pajamas and winter jackets at bedtime and snuggled to keep warm. It never felt as cold, however, as the freezing winters in Corcoran, California, where my family and I picked cotton and lived in a one-room cabin without heat. We slept with our clothes on and huddled together on a wide mattress that lay on the floor.

A few days before Christmas, Laura and I braved the snowy weather and walked cautiously down slippery Grymes Hill to take the bus to the A&P, where we bought a four-foot-tall Christmas tree on sale. We placed it next to the dining table and decorated it with strands of popcorn. On Christmas morning after Mass, Laura and I exchanged gifts: she gave me a thick wool sweater that her maternal grandmother had knitted, and I gave her a small, intricately carved wooden box that I had found at a small shop in lower Manhattan. Three weeks later, for her birthday, I surprised her with a ceramic figurine of a boy leaning against a trash can with a sign that read WITHOUT YOU, I AM DOWN IN THE DUMPS. Both gifts made her very happy. Laura, like my mother, always found joy in everything.

One Step Closer

Our life on Grymes Hill continued to be hectic, what with working every day of the week, but during spring-semester break I completed the 221-page thesis, submitted it to Professor Iduarte, and signed up for the M.A. oral and written exams scheduled for mid-May. Two weeks later he returned the thesis to me with minor changes and asked me to make the revisions and prepare it according to the university's format guidelines for master's theses. I had typed so many rough copies of it, cutting and pasting, that I could hardly bear the thought of typing the final draft.

Laura took pity on me and offered to do it. I thanked her but refused, pointing out that she didn't have time and was overworked. She suggested that I pay someone to type it, using funds from my fellowship stipend. "You can make better use of your time studying for your exams," she said firmly. I agreed and was glad I did.

Before I knew it, the day of the exam arrived. On Monday, May 12, 1969, I got up earlier than usual, having spent a restless night thinking about the test that had weighed heavily on my shoulders for so long. I felt nervous but eager to get it over with. After getting ready, Laura and I said goodbye. "Don't worry about the test," she said. "I'll say a little prayer for you."

"Thanks, I'll need it."

"I have no doubt you'll do great."

Her confidence in me was reassuring. Even if I failed, she would be there for me. "I hope your classes go well," I said. "Please remind my AP class that I won't be there today."

I arrived at Columbia just in time to take the exam, which began at nine o'clock in the Casa Hispánica, the scholarly and cultural center for Hispanic studies, at West 116th Street. The five-hour written exam consisted of ten essay questions on both Latin American and Spanish Peninsular literature, focusing on literary movements; a few questions on the history of the Spanish language; and identification of several major authors and literary critics. I was drained by three o'clock when the exam ended, but felt sure that I had done well.

Four days later I took the one-hour oral exam at ten a.m. in the conference room on the third floor of Philosophy Hall. I felt uneasy as soon as I entered the room and saw Professor James Shearer at the head of the table flanked by Professors Iduarte and Jungmann, who sat across from each other. After we exchanged greetings, Shearer asked me to take the seat at the far end of the table, facing him. "It's the hot seat," he said jokingly. I wasn't amused; it made me more apprehensive. Noticing my nervousness, Professor Iduarte glanced at his colleagues and said, "Francisco's thesis on Gregorio López y Fuentes is excellent." He turned to me and added, "As were your written exams. *Felicitaciones.*" Shearer and Jungmann nodded in agreement and congratulated me also. I felt relieved.

Iduarte proceeded to ask me questions about Mexican writers who were contemporaries of López y Fuentes. I mentioned a few names and elaborated on their importance in Mexican literature. Iduarte smiled approvingly, as did Shearer when I answered his questions about Spanish Peninsular authors. Professor Jungmann frowned when I stumbled over the answer to a question he asked related to the book *Historia de la lengua española*, History of the Spanish Language by Rafael Lapesa, an authority on the Spanish language. Jungmann rephrased the question, guided me through it, and seemed satisfied with the rest of my response.

At the end of the hour I was asked to step outside for a few minutes while they deliberated. I paced up and down the hall, waiting impatiently. Finally Professor Shearer opened the door halfway, stuck out his head, and said, "You may come back in now." When I entered, he and Professors Iduarte and Jungmann stood behind their chairs, smiling. I knew then that I had made it. Each of them congratulated me and shook my hand. I thanked them and floated out of the room, feeling as happy and proud as I did on the day I graduated from college. I exited Philosophy Hall, passed the statue of *The Thinker*, and hurried to Hartley Hall to call Laura to tell her the news, but I quickly realized that she was still at Notre Dame teaching and wouldn't be home.

I left Columbia a little before noon, hoping to surprise her in person, took the subway down to the Battery Park Ferry Terminal, and boarded the Staten Island Ferry. I went up the stairs to the far end of the main level to get the best view of the Statue of Liberty and Ellis Island. As the boat pulled away, I thought of the millions of immigrants who, like Laura's grandparents, had left their homeland and passed through Ellis Island before embarking on a new life in the United States; and I thought of my own family, who, like many others, had crossed the U.S.-Mexican border. I felt grateful for the sacrifices our families made. Their courage and hard work made it possible for her and me to enjoy a good life. We were the heirs of their dreams.

When I got home, I found a sign that Laura had taped to the front door. CONGRATULATIONS, it read. I AM PROUD OF YOU!

A Novice

I spent the summer reading for my comprehensive doctoral exams. Occasionally Laura and I visited museums and did some sightseeing in Manhattan, and life on Grymes Hill the second year started out basically the same as the first year for us. But it soon changed.

Laura was asked to teach a marriage course for seniors instead of Spanish IV, and I became increasingly eager to get a full-time job, especially after my class for nurses was canceled.

The pilot program for teaching Spanish to nurses did not work out. As time went by, the number of students in the class diminished, owing, in part, to their work schedule, which changed every week. The lack of consistency was as frustrating to them as it was to me. They could not attend class on a regular basis, and I had to make on-the-spot adjustments to lesson plans at the beginning of every class to accommodate their needs. By the end of the year, few students were attending, so the program was not renewed.

"I feel I am watching the world go by, and I am not in it," I told Laura. "Besides teaching the AP class, all I do is study. I think about how much more others are doing; they are contributing. I have done nothing; I have contributed nothing."

"That's not true," she said. "Think of what you've done and how you've changed these past three years at Columbia. You finished your master's and the course work for your doctorate. Your professional life is just beginning, and just as life is made up of single days, so are accomplishments. They come in little steps, and each little step leads to your goal. You need to be more patient with yourself."

I listened to her wisdom and decided to get a part-time teaching job and prepare for the doctoral comprehensive exams, which I planned to take at the end of the second semester.

I applied to several local colleges and universities, including Columbia. I received offers from Wagner College in Staten Island and Queensborough Community College in Queens, New York. Columbia offered me a preceptorship, a teaching position available on a competitive basis to graduate students who were one or two years from being awarded the doctorate. The offer included teaching four courses a year, two per semester, tuition exemption, and a salary of $4,200, beginning that fall. The one-year appointment was in the School of General Studies, one of the two undergraduate liberal arts colleges at Columbia.

Known for its nontraditional and international students,

General Studies offered a B.A. degree and a wide variety of courses, which attracted students from Columbia College, the School of Engineering and Applied Science, Barnard College, and the School of Graduate Studies. About half of the classes were offered in the evening to accommodate students and professionals who worked during the day.

I considered the pros and cons of each offer and, with Laura's advice, decided in favor of the preceptorship because I would be in a familiar environment and working with professors whom I knew. Before I could accept the offer, however, I needed to get authorization from the Graduate Faculties Office of Admissions and Financial Aid. I had been awarded a second National Defense Foreign Language Fellowship for 1969–1970, which stipulated that "a fellow may not accept another University appointment, e.g., a Preceptorship or a Teaching or Research Assistantship, without prior written permission."

I wrote to the director of financial aid, asking permission to have both the NDFL Fellowship and the preceptorship, explaining that working was a matter of pride for me and that I wished to continue helping my parents and siblings financially. Several days later I received approval from the Committee on Financial Aid.

Laura and I were delighted. I immediately made an appointment to see Professor Anthony Tudisco, chair of the Spanish Department in the School of General Studies. I met with him in his office in Lewisohn Hall. A tall, solidly built man in his late fifties, he spoke with self-assurance when he congratulated me on being granted the preceptorship and asked, "Is the University of Santa Clara part of the University of California system?"

"No. It's a private Jesuit Catholic university. It's easily confused because several UC campuses have saint's names."

"I see," he said, frowning.

Was he surprised or disappointed? I wasn't sure.

He stood up and asked me to follow him to another office at the end of the hall. "I want you to speak with Susana Redondo de Feldman; she'll work out a teaching schedule for you," he said. "I understand you and she have already met."

"Yes, last year," I said. "I took an advanced writing class with her."

"She is a remarkable woman," he said.

I agreed. I had admired Professor Redondo de Feldman ever since I had completed her course and Professor Iduarte told me about her.

She was born and raised in Cuba, earned a Ph.D. in pedagogy at the University of Havana, and moved to New York in 1944. Knowing little English, she struggled to survive. She took a factory job sewing toy clowns for a time before landing a job as a secretary in the Graduate Spanish Department at Columbia. She took courses at Columbia at night, earned her second Ph.D., taught Spanish part-time, and eventually became a tenured professor.

The door to her office was open. She was sitting at her

desk, writing. As soon as she saw us, she stood up and said cheerfully, *"Entren, entren, que gusto me da verlos!"* Come in, come in, I am so happy to see you. She had almond-shaped eyes and brown skin, and as usual, her shiny black hair was pulled back in a bun. Her friendly, energetic personality was infectious.

Tudisco excused himself and left.

"Please have a seat," she said. "I am so happy you'll be teaching for us."

"Thank you, I am too. It's a privilege." I pulled out a chair and sat across from her.

Professor Redondo de Feldman described the Spanish program and handed me my teaching schedule for the fall semester. I would be teaching two courses three times a week, Mondays, Wednesdays, and Fridays: Elementary Spanish Grammar, Reading, and Conversation; and Intermediate Spanish, General Review of Grammar, with Emphasis on Self-expression. She gave me the syllabus and a list of textbooks and readers I was to use for each class. "I hope this schedule is okay with you," she said.

I felt my jaw tightening. Recalling my father's advice to always accept work unconditionally and be grateful to have a job, I resisted telling her that I preferred teaching two sections of the same course, which would give me only one preparation. I also thought it would be disrespectful, as she had been my professor.

"It's fine, thank you," I responded.

I left her office feeling welcomed and acknowledged but worried about teaching at Columbia.

I spent hours studying Spanish grammar and thinking about how best to teach my two courses. I was determined not only to learn the material well but also to teach it effectively. So I enrolled in a graduate class that semester at Columbia Teachers College on teaching methods, and I asked Laura for guidance, as she had taught Spanish under supervision during her graduate studies and had taught at Notre Dame Academy for more than a year.

Even though I was prepared, I was extremely nervous the day I was to teach my first college class. I left for Columbia right after my AP Spanish literature class, ate a snack on the way, and arrived on campus in late morning. I went to Butler Library and spent over an hour reviewing my lesson plans and jotting down on a three-by-five card what I was going to say and do at the beginning of class. At one o'clock I left the library and headed to Hamilton Hall, where my class was held. I entered the lobby, and as I climbed the marble stairs to room 303, I felt my legs trembling and my heart pounding. I slowly opened the classroom door, slipped in, and placed my briefcase on a small table in front of the room. I introduced myself and greeted the students, who filled every seat. I could feel my hands shaking as I distributed copies of the course syllabus. "As you can tell, I am a bit nervous," I said apologetically. "This is my first time teaching a college class." Polite laughter and friendly smiles filled the room, which eased my tension. I took attendance and asked the students to introduce themselves. Most were pursuing a first or second college degree; others were international graduate students or working professionals: lawyers, accountants, actors, journalists, and military veterans—all eager to learn Spanish.

Before I knew it, the class was over. I ended up being overly prepared and did not cover the whole lesson. I was disappointed and tired. I did slightly better in my second class, but not as well as I had expected.

On the ferry back to Staten Island late that evening, I replayed in my mind my experience in both classes and made mental notes on what I could have done differently. I arrived home exhausted and disappointed but determined to do better next time.

After several days of teaching and preparing lessons, I noticed that the Spanish-language textbook we were using included cultural units on Spain and Latin America, but not on Spanish-speaking communities in the United States. Capitalizing on my students' immediate experience with the Spanish spoken by Hispanics living in New York City, I taught them vocabulary and idiomatic expressions unique to Puerto Ricans and Cubans, as well as to Mexicans living in the West and Southwest. I emphasized that the students should value and learn those linguistic variations along with "standard Spanish." I also taught them about the rich cultural heritage of Hispanics in the United States.

Teaching at the university level was hard work and time-consuming but most rewarding. I met with many of my students individually outside of class to help them increase their oral proficiency and to get to know them better. Our discussions were enthusiastic and frank, which made teaching and learning more personal, more relaxed and enjoyable. I found it most gratifying to see them make progress in speaking Spanish and become increasingly interested in learning not only about Hispanic life and culture in Latin America and Spain but also in the United States. I felt I was helping them gain a better understanding of and appreciation for our culturally diverse society. There was no doubt in my mind that teaching was my vocation.

Within Reach

I felt ready. A year had passed since I had completed my master's degree and course work for the Ph.D., and now I was set to take my comprehensive exams for the doctorate. I filled out the petition and went to see Professor Shearer in his office for his approval and signature. After looking at my academic record carefully and signing the petition, he said, "Looks like everything is in order. Good luck."

I thanked him and waited for him to say something about the exam, anything that would help me better prepare for it. He stared at me as though wondering why I was still standing there. I broke the awkward silence and asked, "Could you please give me some idea of what area or areas the exam will focus on?"

"You must know and be able to evaluate critically Spanish literature from the time of Adam and Eve to the present," he said, chuckling.

I felt blood rushing to my face and my heart pounding.

"Seriously," he said. "Focus on your field of specialization, Latin American literature. However, you should have a general knowledge of Spanish Peninsular literature too."

I was relieved but annoyed and frustrated by his humor. I feigned a smile, thanked him, and left.

The comprehensive written exams were not as difficult as I thought. I was given two long take-home essays: one on Simón Bolívar's letters to the Ecuadorian poet José Joaquín Olmedo and one on Mariano Azuela's classic novel *Los de abajo*.

A week after I turned in my essays, which I passed successfully, I took the oral exam with Professors Shearer, Iduarte, Jungemann, and Sobejano in the department's conference room. I felt less nervous and more confident than I did when I took the orals for the master's, as I had already gone through the process once and was better prepared. Once again, I sat at the end of the long, rectangular table facing Professor Shearer, who presided over the exam; Professors Jungemann and Iduarte sat on my right, facing Sobejano on my left. Each of them took turns firing questions based on their own areas of expertise, which meant that half of the exam dealt with Spanish Peninsular literature, one-fourth with Latin American literature, and the rest with the history of the Spanish language. They seemed pleased with my performance, especially Jungmann, whose questions I answered correctly, without hesitation. "You did much better this time!" he said.

The exam lasted an hour and a half, and after it was over, I was asked to step out of the room while the faculty deliberated. Within minutes, Professor Shearer came out and asked me to return.

"You are now a certified Ph.D. candidate," Professor Shearer said. "Congratulations."

When I first arrived at Columbia, he had told me that as far as the department was concerned, I did not exist until I had passed the doctoral comprehensive exams. I felt like telling him, *I am not invisible anymore*, but simply said, "Thank you. I'm glad it's over."

Professor Iduarte gave me a warm hug and whispered in my ear, *"Excelente, Panchito."*

"Gracias a usted." Thanks to you, I responded.

Laura and I celebrated. We had a steak dinner with a glass of wine at home and enjoyed a delicious chocolate cake she had baked. The next day, we splurged and went to Manhattan to see García Lorca's play *The House of Bernarda Alba*, which was playing off-Broadway.

Now that I was a doctoral candidate, I faced the daunting task, with Professor Iduarte's guidance, of selecting a topic for my dissertation. I felt overwhelmed by the idea of writing a book-length study that had to be original and contribute to my field of concentration. Before meeting with Professor Iduarte, however, I wanted to have a clear idea about what I wanted to research. I recalled that several older graduate students in the Spanish Ph.D. program had been working on their doctoral dissertations for several years and were still not finished. I looked for a topic that would excite and engage me over time, knowing that it would take many, many months to do the research and many more to do the writing. I spent days thinking about specific themes and authors I had studied. The course on the literature of the Mexican Revolution, which in part dealt with the identity of Mexico and its struggle to come to terms with its indigenous past, kept coming to mind.

Prior to the Revolution, the Indians suffered injustices and were left out of Mexico's mainstream social order and culture. The society was not inclusive. I compared that unfortunate reality to the history and segregation of blacks and Mexicans and the discrimination against them in our own country. It was clear that the United States was not an inclusive and just society either. I thought of my experiences in grammar school, high school, and college, and I asked: Were there any groups missing from the literature we studied during that time? As I considered the question, the answer became clear: blacks and Mexican Americans and other minorities were either not included or not well represented in any of the literary works we read in school. I thought of the dramatic skits performed by the Teatro Campesino during César Chávez's march to Sacramento and their later performances in New York City in support of the grape boycott in California. As result, I became intensely interested in doing my dissertation on some aspect of Mexican American literature. I wanted to explore and study works written by Mexicans and their descendants living or having lived in the United States who wrote about their experience in our country.

I went to see Professor Iduarte during his office hours on Wednesday, after teaching my afternoon class, and proposed the topic to him. He was sympathetic but discouraged me from pursuing it. He felt that the university would not consider the subject a legitimate topic of study. He pointed out that even Latin American literature (literature of the Spanish-speaking countries of the Western Hemisphere) was not considered a subject suitable for a Ph.D. at Columbia until the 1920s. Up until then, only doctoral dissertations in Spanish Peninsular literature (literature of Spain) were accepted. To my dismay, I later discovered that this bias was common among doctoral-granting institutions nationwide.

I was deeply disappointed and troubled, but I appreciated and respected his advice. As an alternative, he suggested writing my dissertation on Victoriano Salado Álvarez's historical novels, *Episodios nacionales mexicanos*, National Mexican Episodes. When I told him that I knew very little about this Mexican author, Professor Iduarte proceeded to tell me that Salado was born in Teocaltiche, a small town a few miles north of San Pedro Tlaquepaque, the place where I was born in the state of Jalisco. This caught my attention. He indicated that Salado had published a collection of short stories and numerous books on various subjects, ranging from literary criticism to Mexican history, but his best-known work was the *Episodios nacionales mexicanos*, a history of Mexico in novel form, covering the period from Santa Anna's rule to the end of the French intervention, 1851–1867. "No one has done a study on this important work," he said. This piqued my interest even more.

Since Mexican history and literature were two passions of mine, I agreed with Professor Iduarte's recommendation. He was pleased. As I was leaving his office, he said, "I am sure you'll enjoy reading the *Episodios*, Panchito. I read them when I was in the *preparatoria*. They got me interested in history."

On Saturday afternoon Laura and I went to the Americas Bookstore in Manhattan to look for a copy of Salado's *Episodios nacionales mexicanos*. I was not optimistic about finding it, because the first edition was out of print, and according to Professor Iduarte, the only other edition, published in 1945, was rare.

I had been to the store several times to buy books for my classes. The old, musty space had wall-to-wall shelves jampacked with books on top of books, many covered with dust. There were stacks and stacks of paperbacks and hardbacks everywhere, including in the aisles, which made it difficult to get around. They seemed not to be placed in any particular order. However, Mr. Molina, the owner, appeared to know exactly what books he had and generally where they were located. I asked him if he had the *Episodios*.

"Look around. I think I have a copy," he said. "I'll be right with you." He adjusted his baggy pants, rolled up his shirtsleeves, and climbed onto a stack of books, reaching to get a volume from a top shelf for an impatient customer. There were several people ahead of us who were also waiting for him.

Laura and I began our search. We spent a long time plowing through hundreds of dusty books but found nothing. Mr. Molina finally joined us in our hunt.

"I know they're here somewhere," he said.

Several minutes later I heard Laura's faint voice coming from behind one of the tall, freestanding bookshelves: "*Epi-so-dios na-cion-ales . . .*"

"You're kidding. Don't fool around," I said loudly.

She came around the corner, smiling from ear to ear and holding in her hand volume one of the *Episodios*. She had found the fourteen-volume paperback second edition, published in 1945. Laura and I hugged each other.

"I can't tell who's happier—you or your wife," Mr. Molina said, laughing.

I purchased the collection for thirty dollars. That evening I read the first half of volume one, wrote notes in the margins of every page, and underlined passages.

It was only the beginning.

A New Life

Our plan to start a family two years after getting married fell into place once I passed the Ph.D. comprehensive exams. At the recommendation of Professors Tudisco and Redondo de Feldman, I was promoted to instructor, teaching full-time in the School of General Studies, which doubled my salary and qualified me for Columbia faculty housing near the university. My mother and siblings were doing better financially. Trampita was returning home from the army safe and sound; Torito had finished his associate of arts degree at Hancock College and continued working part-time as a custodian while attending Cal Poly in San Luis Obispo; my mother was now employed at St. Mary's Hospital as a nurse's aide; and Ruben and Rorra, both in high school, worked in the fields on weekends. My father's health was improving. He had finally gone to see a doctor about his stomach problems and had a tumor the size of an egg removed from his large intestine. Even though he continued to suffer from headaches and back problems, he managed to help Tía Chana and her husband sell masonry materials out of their *corral*, backyard. Laura and I could now afford to have a child without both of us having to work outside the home, and we would continue to help my family as best we could. Laura left her teaching position at Notre Dame Academy at the end of the school year, and that summer we moved to upper Manhattan. I no longer had to commute three hours a day.

We left a green and peaceful island and moved into a noisy, grimy, densely populated one covered in concrete and surrounded by students, professors, and poor and elderly people living in rent-controlled high-rise apartments. It was unsafe to walk alone at night on Broadway from 116th Street to Ninety-sixth. Signs posted at the entrance to Morningside Park read HIGH CRIME AREA. ENTER AT YOUR OWN RISK.

Our new home was an apartment in an old four-story building at 608 West 113th Street, between Broadway and Riverside Drive. It measured approximately five hundred square feet and was on the first floor, a few feet back from the two-door entrance to the building. It had a kitchenette, a bathroom, and a living room that had been divided in half to create a bedroom. The bedroom had a tiny side window, which looked onto the red-brick wall of the adjacent apartment building, and a door that opened out to a small cement backyard that had so many cracks it looked like a gray road map. The living room window, with bars attached, had a view of the back of a tall apartment building that cast a shadow like a gloomy dark cloud.

Laura and I cleaned the apartment and made it as spotless as we could. She washed the greasy kitchen walls, stove, shelves, and countertops, and I scrubbed the toilet with cleanser and steel wool. I borrowed a floor-scrubbing machine from the university's housekeeping office, and to our surprise, under the filth was a nice dark brown cork floor. Laura lined the kitchen shelves and covered the area behind the stove with floral design contact paper, and we filled in the gaps around water pipes with extra-fine steel wool to prevent cockroaches from creeping in.

Two weeks after we had settled in, on the tenth of July, Laura came home from seeing the doctor. She was beaming. "I am pregnant! The test came back positive. We're going to have a baby!" She could hardly keep still.

"We're going to have a baby!" I exclaimed. Laura and I embraced and kissed and jumped up and down like silly children on a trampoline. I felt pure, soaring joy.

"I wonder what our baby will look like," I said after calming down. "I hope it has big brown eyes like yours." I felt an intense passion of caring and love for her and our child.

We immediately called our families to tell them the great news, and later that day I sent a letter to her grandparents: *When Laura told me she was expecting*, I wrote, *she looked like she had been to heaven . . . The thought of being the father to her child makes me very proud and happy.*

After going through many possible Spanish names, we came up with two: Cecilia if a girl and Francisco Andrés if a boy, in honor of my father and Professor Andrés Iduarte.

Laura's pregnancy went smoothly. She had unending energy and enthusiasm for doing things. She took a sewing class at Riverside Church and made her own maternity clothes and curtains for the windows. She took care of household chores and monthly finances, sending money to my mother and father and putting twenty-five dollars in our savings account whenever possible. She cooked special meals for some of my students who could not go home for the holidays, and she read scholarly articles to me for my dissertation research whenever I was too tired to read them myself. Occasionally Professor Iduarte and his wife, Graciela, also came over for dinner, and sometimes they invited us to their home with Professor Redondo de Feldman and her husband, Kenney.

On Monday March 8, 1971, I was sound asleep when suddenly I felt Laura pull back the bed covers. "What's wrong?" I asked, wiping my eyes with the back of my hand and glancing at the clock. It was six a.m.

"I think it's time," she said.

I jumped out of bed, turned on the light, and quickly started to get dressed. "I'll call a cab while you get ready."

"Don't get a cab. We'll walk," she said. "The hospital is only three blocks away."

"Yeah, three long blocks."

We bundled up and rushed out the door. It was freezing

cold. We walked cautiously half a block on the snow-covered sidewalk to the corner of 113th and Broadway, and over Laura's objection, I hailed a cab. "To St. Luke's Women's Hospital on One Hundred Fourteenth Street and Amsterdam," I said.

The driver made a face. "It's only two blocks away," he said under his breath.

After being admitted, Laura was put in the maternity ward. I kept her company and coached her through her contractions as they became more and more frequent. Dr. Panayotopoulos, her obstetrician, an imposing woman, came in periodically to check on Laura's progress. Time dragged on and on. Finally, at six thirty in the evening she was taken into the delivery room. Dr. Panayotopoulos handed me a mask and gown and asked me to put it on and step out into the hallway. "I'll call you in when she's ready to deliver." I waited impatiently, pacing up and down the corridor. I kept looking at my watch, wondering why it was taking so long. Was she all right?

After about twenty endless minutes Dr. Panayotopoulos came out of the delivery room. "You can come in now. Congratulations! It's a boy." I was elated but confused and disappointed that I did not see him being born. "I am terribly sorry I didn't call you in earlier. I forgot you were out here waiting," she added when she noticed my puzzlement and displeasure.

I was taken by emotion when I saw Laura lying in bed with

our baby on her chest. She looked exhausted but radiant and contented. "It's our boy," she said. "Isn't he beautiful?"

He had short legs, a long torso, and a head full of bright red hair. "He is." I felt an all-consuming love I had never experienced before. Laura and I kissed and cried with happiness. Our lives had changed forever.

Crossing the Line

Even though I was not able to do my Ph.D. dissertation on Mexican American literature, the opportunity to work on that topic came up when several Mexican American undergraduate students from Columbia College came to my office and asked if I could offer them a class on Mexican American literature and culture in the fall semester. Thrilled at the possibility, I told them that I would have to check with the administration and that I would be willing to guide them only in research projects, using a seminar or independent study format because I was not well versed in the subject. "It'll be a collaborative effort," I said. "We'll learn together." They agreed and were enthusiastic to enroll in the class.

Based on the discussion Professor Iduarte and I had had about selecting a topic for my dissertation, I anticipated resistance from the administration, so I worked extra hard in designing a syllabus for the course.

I met with Professor Redondo in her office and discussed the study plan and idea for the new class. Initially she seemed reluctant because I was scheduled to teach an intermediate Spanish class and a survey course on Hispanic literature. "Let me check the schedule," she said. This was a good sign. "I think we can make adjustments," she said, looking at me over her reading glasses and smiling.

"I can't thank you enough, *Profesora*," I said. "The students will be very happy."

"Don't count on it yet," she said. "I need to submit this plan to Professor Michael Riffaterre for his approval. I have an appointment to see him tomorrow morning. I'll discuss it with him then."

Michael Riffaterre was professor of French in the Department of French and Romance Philology and was appointed interim chairman of the Department of Spanish and Portuguese Studies.

The next day, I went to see Professor Redondo de Feldman, eager to know the decision. "Professor Riffaterre was skeptical," she said, "but he said he would think about it and get back to us."

"Thank you very much, *Profesora*," I said. I was disappointed, but not surprised, and remained cautiously hopeful.

Two days later I received a letter from Professor Riffaterre through intercampus mail. It read:

After consultation with my colleagues, I should like to inform you that the Spanish Department will allow you to teach on your own time and without financial compensation a course on the literature of Mexican Americans.

This course should not be taken for credit nor could it be included in our official Bulletin. I am sure you understand that these restrictions are advisable in view of the very tentative nature of this experiment. I have no doubt however, that its best hope to succeed is the fact that you will be teaching it.

I was glad he had endorsed the class, but angry at his terms, which I interpreted as an attempt to discourage me. I immediately sent him a response through intercampus mail, with copies to Professor Redondo, Professor Iduarte, and the dean of the college. I wrote:

Thank you, Professsor Riffaterre, for approving the course. I accept all your conditions except one: that the course should not be taken for credit. I feel that it is unfair and unjust to expect students to do the work and not give them credit for it. I would appreciate it if you would reconsider this restriction.

Professor Redondo and Professor Iduarte called to tell me that they had read my letter and had contacted the dean of the college to advise him to approve my course for credit. "Thank you," I told them. "Your support, no matter the outcome, means a lot to me."

Two days later I received a copy of a letter that Michael Rosenthal, the associate dean of the college, wrote to Professor Riffaterre. It read:

As there has been much confusion surrounding the establishment by Chicano students of an independent study course this term with Mr. Jimenez, I think it reasonable to put in writing what my current understanding is. I am all in favor of Mr. Jimenez taking on students for independent study in Mexican-American literature, with the syllabus, the specific projects, and the grades all coming under his jurisdiction. The course would be for three points and would be included under the already existing category of the Latin American Seminar C3812y. Special arrangements will be made for this course to be taken for three points instead of the four listed in the catalogue. If Mr. Jimenez will submit to me a list of the students, I will take care of this.

I hope this view bears some relationship to the facts of what will actually happen. Thanks for putting up with much unnecessary trouble.

I was insulted by the cynical tone of the letter, especially the last paragraph, but I was pleased with the end result. I went to see Professors Iduarte and Redondo de Feldman to share the news and to thank them personally for their help.

Even though I taught the Mexican American literature class without financial compensation and on my own time, the rewards were many. Besides working with talented students and learning from them, I conducted research on sources and themes in this body of work, focusing on the Teatro Campesino, the Chicano theatrical troupe founded by Luis Valdez in 1965 to support César Chávez's efforts to unionize farm workers. I also cofounded *The Bilingual Review/La revista bilingüe*, a scholarly journal and literary magazine. Although it focused primarily on bilingualism, the publication also served as an outlet for creative writers whose works dealt with Hispanic themes relating particularly to Hispanic life in the United States.

At end of that fall semester I met with Professor Iduarte in his office for the third time that term to talk about my dissertation research.

"*¿Cómo están Laura y Pancholín?*" he asked.

Professor Iduarte gave our son the nickname Pancholín because Pancho is the nickname for Francisco and "lín" sounded Italian and musical.

"They're doing fine, thank you. Pancholín is a bundle of energy and is beginning to crawl. He likes it when we put him in the stroller and take him on walks around campus. He loves being around people."

"I am glad to hear it," he said. "Sounds like his mom."

He paused and turned his attention to my research. "I have some information that will help you on your dissertation," he said. He reached into his desk drawer, took out a folded piece of paper, handed it to me, and added, "This is Salado Álvarez's granddaughter's address in Mexico City. She has all of his papers. I've written to her about you and your research. You should contact her."

"I will, thank you," I said.

"By the way, Professor Redondo shared with me a piece you wrote for her advanced Expression and Style class about a migrant child who yearns to receive a red ball for Christmas. It's very moving."

"Thank you," I said, feeling emotional and proud. "It's based on a personal experience."

"*Así me lo imaginaba.*" I thought so. He leaned forward in his chair and added, "*Cuéntame más de esas experiencias.*" Tell me more about those experiences.

I briefly told him about my family crossing the border illegally, all of us working in the fields, missing school, my father's illness, and passing my janitorial job on to my younger sibling so that, with financial aid, I could attend the University of Santa Clara, where I took on a few part-time jobs to pay for personal expenses and to send money home.

"This is fascinating. You should write your story and publish it!" he said emphatically. He reached out and placed his hand on my shoulder and gave me an intense, caring look. "You must."

I was touched and surprised by his suggestion. "When I was in college, I began to jot down memories of my childhood," I said, "but have not written anything systematically."

"That's a good start," he said, pulling out a small book from the shelf. The title was *Un niño en la Revolución Mexicana*, A Child in the Mexican Revolution. "It's an autobiography of when I was a boy during the Mexican Revolution," he explained. "I was living with Rómulo Gallegos and Gabriela Mistral and other writers in Spain in the midst of the Spanish Civil War when I started writing it." He picked up his pen, signed the copy, and handed it to me. "Here. I hope this encourages you to write your own story."

I was deeply moved by his gift and his advice. He reminded me of my sophomore high school English teacher, Miss Bell, who told me I had writing talent after reading an essay I wrote for her class about my younger brother Trampita.

Thanks to Professor Iduarte's encouragement, I went back to my notes and reworked two pieces, *"Muerte Fría,"* Cold Death, and *"Un Aguinaldo,"* A Christmas Gift. As I was writing, I realized that my story was not unique. There were many families and their children who had gone through experiences similar to the ones my family and I had lived through.

I then recalled César Chávez's speech, about justice and human dignity, at the end of the march to Sacremento. "If you are outraged at conditions, then you cannot possibly be free or happy until you devote all your time to changing them and do nothing but that," he said. "Fighting for social justice, it seems to me, is one of the profoundest ways in which men can say *yes* to human dignity and that really means sacrifice. The best source of power, the best source of hope, is straight from you, the people." When I first heard that speech, I had looked at the banner of the Virgen de Gaudalupe and, feeling deeply the suffering and pain of migrant workers, asked myself, *What can and should I do in my life to help them?* I did not have the answer then. But now I did. I would write to document part of my family's history and, more important, to chronicle the lives of many migrant families from the past and present and draw attention to their plight.

I sent the two vignettes to *El Grito: Journal of Contempo-*

rary Mexican-American Thought, a literary journal published by Quinto Sol Publications in Berkeley, California. I had come across it while doing research for my class on Mexican American literature. I also wrote a rough draft of another piece, *"La mudanza,"* The Move, which I later titled "The Circuit."

Laura and I were ecstatic when I received a letter from the editor informing me that both works were accepted for publication in *Prosa Chicana Contemporánea/Contemporary Chicano Prose*, a special issue of *El Grito*, which also included writings by Rudolfo Anaya, Rolando Hinojosa, Estela Portillo de Trambley, and Tomás Rivera. It was scheduled to appear in the spring of the following year. This wonderful news gave me confidence and increased my desire to continue writing autobiographical pieces. However, knowing that I had to have a Ph.D. and produce a body of scholarly research and publications if I were to earn tenure at Columbia or elsewhere, I set aside writing stories about my childhood and turned my attention to completing my dissertation.

In Hand

Early in the summer, when Pancholín was three months
old, we visited Laura's and my families so they could
meet him and so that we could have him baptized. Roberto
and Darlene, who did us the honor of being the godparents,
made all the arrangements for the religious ceremony in
Santa Maria's St. Mary of the Assumption Catholic Church
and hosted a reception for family and friends at their home.
Everyone, especially my mother, doted on Pancholín. She
was amazed at his thick, deep red hair. *"Tal vez se parece a tu
papá cuando era niño."* Perhaps he looks like your dad when
he was a child, our mother said, sitting on a sofa and holding
Pancholín in her arms. *"Le decían el güero."* They used to call
him the blond one.

"I remember our father telling us that," I said, "but I think
Pancholín's features are more like Laura's. He has big eyes,
long eyelashes, and thin lips."

Our mother gazed at Pancholín and then looked up at

Laura, who was sitting across from her. "You know, I think you're right," she said.

During our four-day stay with my brother and his wife, Laura and I had fun being with their cute eighteen-month-old son, Robert Anthony, and their beautiful daughters Jackie, Angela, and Laura. They were close in age and played together. Watching them started us thinking about having a second child in a year or two. We wanted our children to grow up together and have fond memories of each other as they became older.

Laura and I returned to New York at the end of June. I had been appointed to serve a two-year term on the Scholarship Committee for the School of General Studies, which met early in July for five consecutive days. After completing the task of selecting scholarship recipients, I spent the rest of the summer writing my dissertation in my cubicle office in Lewisohn Hall, an air-conditioned building. Laura would bring Pancholín to my office in a stroller to escape the blistering and humid heat in our apartment. She would entertain him while he was awake, and when he napped, she read for enjoyment.

I dedicated most of my time that academic year to teaching and writing and serving on the Casa Hispánica Committee, which brought such renowned scholars and writers as Enrique Anderson Imbert, Jorge Luis Borges, Octavio Paz, and Mario Vargas Llosa to make presentations or do readings in the Casa Hispánica.

It was a lonely and isolating experience working on the dissertation in my office every day between classes and committee meetings and on weekends. And even though I enjoyed doing research and learning and discovering new ideas, I felt guilty for not spending more time with my family.

I always looked forward to going home in the evenings after work and seeing Laura and Pancholín. No matter how busy and stressful a day I had, they always made me feel better. I loved seeing the joy on Pancholín's face when Laura and I smiled at him. I would pick him up and hold him and kiss him and tickle him. His big, hearty giggle warmed my heart, and when he lay on my chest and absent-mindedly stroked my shoulder gently with his tiny hand, I felt blessed.

In the summer of the following year, early July of 1972, we got wonderful news: Laura was expecting. We were just as jubilant then as we were when we found out that she was pregnant with Pancholín, and so were our families and close friends and colleagues. The baby was due the first week in February. We chose the names Cecilia if a girl and Miguel Antonio if a boy.

Professor Redondo de Feldman came to my office and gave me a card signed by everyone in the department. "With a growing family, you need a bigger apartment," she said. I agreed with her and told her that we had no options because of the short supply of apartments and high rents. She proceeded to tell me that her friend Leonardo de Morelos, who taught at Columbia College for many years, had retired, and he and his wife wished to sublet their large, fully furnished apartment for one year. They were returning to Mexico, their native land, but were not sure whether they would stay, so they wanted to hold on to the apartment. "It's right across the street from Columbia. Are you interested?" she asked.

"Of course," I said. "Thank you for telling me. It would be great if we could we get it."

"I've already told Leonardo and his wife about you and Laura and Pancholín," she said. "I think you can count on it."

Laura was thrilled when I told her about it, and we went to see Professor de Morelos at his apartment on the fifth floor of 438 West 116th Street, on the corner of Amsterdam Avenue. I carried Pancholín in a child backpack. Professor de Morelos was a short man in his late sixties. He told us that his wife had already left for Mexico, and he gave us a quick tour of the apartment. It had two bedrooms, a living room with hardwood floors and large windows, a large, fully equipped kitchen, bathroom and tub, and a spacious study with built-in bookshelves and a writing desk. The view from the study was the west corner of Hamilton Hall and the entrance to College Walk. The vista from the living room was Columbia Law School.

Anticipating my question about the rent, de Morelos said, "The monthly payment is only one hundred and seventy-five dollars. It's low because it's rent-controlled. We've been living here since 1954."

Even though $175 was fifteen dollars more per month

than what we were spending for our apartment on 113th Street, Laura and I felt we would be able to handle the extra expense. We signed the one-year lease, moved into our new home at the end of July, and promised the de Moreloses that we would take good care of their apartment and their belongings while they were gone.

Once we had settled in, two weeks into the fall semester, I met Professor Iduarte in his office to discuss the fourth and last chapter of my dissertation, which I had submitted to him in early September when he returned from his summer vacation in Mexico.

"Chapter four is first-rate, just like the other three chapters," Professor Iduarte said, handing it to me. "You're done. Congratulations."

I was delighted, but stunned by what he said next.

"You should plan to defend your dissertation this November. I have already started thinking about putting together the dissertation defense committee."

I couldn't believe my ears. I could feel my face turning red. I was tongue-tied.

"What's the matter?" he asked, giving me a perplexed look. "Aren't you pleased?"

"Oh, I am," I said. "Thank you! It's just that . . . it's so soon. I was planning to defend it at the end of spring semester."

"You can do it, Panchito," he said. "It's to your advantage. If you complete your degree this semester, you'll be promoted to assistant professor at the beginning of next year, in January."

I appreciated Professor Iduarte's enthusiasm and confidence in me. And even though I felt more stress, I agreed with him and settled on a date and time for the defense of my dissertation: November 20 at ten a.m.

When I got home, Laura was sitting on the sofa cuddling Pancholín, who was asleep. I gave them both a kiss and told her about the conversation with Professor Iduarte. "It means I'll be in my office working even more in the evenings and weekends, and spending less time at home with you and Pancholín during the next few weeks," I said apologetically.

"It's great news about your dissertation," she said. "Please don't worry about us. We can make it!"

For the next three weeks I worked harder than ever, making final revisions and proofreading the dissertation. I had it typed according to the university's format guidelines for Ph.D. dissertations, made five copies, and submitted them to Professor Iduarte, who distributed them to members of the committee for review.

The evening of November 19, Professor Iduarte called me at home to see how I was doing. "*No te preocupes, Panchito.*" Don't worry, he said. "*Relájate y duerme bien. Vas a salir muy bien.*" Relax and sleep well. You'll do very well.

His comforting words calmed my nerves, but I had a restless night.

The next morning I felt tense. After a light breakfast I

skimmed through my copy of the dissertation, wondering what questions I might be asked by the committee. I placed it in my briefcase and kissed Laura and Pancholín goodbye. "Do your best," Laura said, giving me a long and warm hug. On my way to the Spanish Department conference room in Philosophy Hall, I said a prayer to the Virgen de Guadalupe.

The conference room door was open when I arrived. Five professors who formed the dissertation defense committee were sitting at the table, each with a copy of the dissertation in front of him. Professor Iduarte greeted me and motioned for me to sit in the chair at the end of the table, closest to the entrance. He introduced two members of the exam committee whom I had not met: Harold Ferrar, an assistant professor of English, and Richard Hofstadter, professor of history. The other two members, besides Professor Iduarte, were Gonzalo Sobejano and Frederick Jungemann (Professor Shearer had retired).

From the start, Professor Hofstadter, who chaired the committee, set a friendly and positive tone. He began by informing me that the committee had already met to discuss my dissertation. "You should know that there is consensus among us that your dissertation is excellent," he said with a slight smile, "so the suggestions we are going to make are aimed at helping you prepare your work for publication." Upon hearing these words, I felt an incredibly heavy burden lift off my shoulders. For the next hour and a half I answered their general questions and specific ones, which focused on each chapter, and wrote down their recommendations for improvement. At the end, Professor Hofstadter and the rest of the committee congratulated me. I thanked each committee member, shaking his hand. Professor Iduarte accompanied me to the door and said, *"Felicitaciones, Panchito, me siento muy orgulloso de ti. Celebraremos más tarde."* I am very proud of you. We'll celebrate later.

I rushed home to tell Laura that we had indeed made it. She and Pancholín greeted me with a surprise chocolate cake. It had a hand-piped inscription that read "Congratulations, Dr. Jiménez." She also gave me two albums, *Sounds of Silence* and *Bridge Over Troubled Water,* by Simon and Garfunkel, whose songs I had enjoyed on the radio during my graduate studies at Columbia.

A half-hour later Professor Iduarte and Graciela and Professor Redondo de Feldman joined us in the celebration. Professor Iduarte brought a bottle of champagne, and Professor Redondo gave me, on behalf of the Spanish Department, a Lladró porcelain figurine of Don Quijote standing and holding a sword. I thanked them and told them that I felt fortunate and blessed. "The Ph.D. belongs to you, my teachers and friends, and to Laura and my family," I said.

For the rest of the day I felt as if I were in a dream. It was hard for me to believe that after six long and hard years of graduate school I was finally finished. I remembered with a smile my mother asking me, year after year, "When are you going to be done with school, *mijo?* You've been in school for so long!" I then thought of my father, who, like my mother, had worked in the fields every day from sunup to sundown to give us a better life. Having completed my doctorate, I felt I had honored, in a small way, my parents' sacrifices and partly fulfilled their dreams. That evening I wrote my father a letter to tell him the good news and to thank him. I wrote a similar letter to my mother. Laura and I included in the letters a picture of Pancholín. I called Roberto and Darlene and thanked them, too.

My doctorate was officially confirmed on Thanksgiving Day, November 23, 1972.

A Wonder

The new year began with multiple gifts: I was promoted to assistant professor, and, most excitingly, our second child was soon to be born.

Laura joined a baby-sitting co-op with neighbors in our building. She took care of Lisa, a little girl the same age as Pancholín, whose parents were practicing attorneys and lived next door. Bert, Lisa's mother, and Laura traded baby-sitting hours; Bert watched Pancholín whenever Laura attended Lamaze classes at St. Luke's or had an appointment to see her doctor, Gerard De Catalogne, a refined, gentle, and courteous man who had emigrated from Haiti to the United States.

As the baby's due date of February 4 drew closer, I would rush home after my classes. Spring semester classes had begun on Monday, January 22. I was teaching Monday, Wednesday, and Friday early afternoons and Tuesday and Thursday evenings. I worried constantly while I was in class that I would not be home in time to take Laura to the hospital. Fortunately, at the end of January, Wanda, Laura's mother, flew to New York to help us with Pancholín and the new baby once it was born. I prayed for the baby's birth to be on a weekend, when I could be home all day.

On a cloudy and chilly Saturday afternoon, February 3, I came home after going to the post office and found Laura sitting on the couch, leaning slightly to her right. Wanda sat on a chair facing her. Pancholín was napping. Before I had a chance to ask Laura how she was doing, she said, "I've started having labor pains, but it's too early to go to the hospital."

"I think you should go now," Wanda said, visibly nervous and looking at me for support.

I sat next to Laura and rubbed her back. "I agree with Wanda. We should go," I said.

"Let's wait just a little while longer," Laura responded calmly. She shifted her body to the left, seeking a more comfortable position.

A half-hour later the contractions became more frequent. "I think we'd better go," Laura said.

I quickly got up, reached out, and grabbed Laura's hand to help her up. Wanda assisted in putting on her dark blue raincoat and black scarf. On the way out, Laura and I slipped into Pancholín's room, leaned over his crib, and kissed him lightly. "You'll soon have a baby brother or sister," I whispered.

Laura and I tiptoed out of his room, said goodbye to Wanda, and headed to St. Luke's, a block from our apartment. Laura leaned on my arm for support as we walked down Amsterdam Avenue. After we checked in at the front desk, Laura was taken to the maternity ward. I was given an orange gown to put on and asked to wait outside. Within minutes the door flew open, and out came a nurse pushing a gurney with Laura lying on it. She looked harried.

"What's wrong?" I asked, panicked.

"Laura is ready to deliver," the nurse said. "I called Dr. De Catalogne. He's on his way. He's in Brooklyn." A second nurse joined in pushing the gurney rapidly down the hall, into the elevator, up to the seventh floor to the delivery room. I followed right behind them, determined to see our baby being born. Once in the delivery room, the nurses prepped her, and Dr. Casanova, a Puerto Rican intern, gave her instructions while I coached her. "When you feel the urge to push, push," he said.

"Now, breathe deeply," I said repeatedly, recalling the Lamaze exercises and holding her hand. This went on for about half an hour. I glanced at the clock on the wall. It was 4:23 p.m.

"One more—push . . . as hard as you can," Dr. Casanova said.

I could see the baby's head. As Laura pushed again and gave the loudest and most powerful scream I had ever heard, our baby was born. The doctor held it up and said, "It's a boy. Congratulations, Mom and Dad."

"A boy!" I cried out, shaking with excitement. "It's a boy."

"Another son," Laura said, smiling from ear to ear. Her big eyes were full of tears.

After Dr. Casanova had me cut the umbilical cord, the nurse took the baby, washed him, and laid him on Laura's chest. "Our lovely Miguelito," Laura said, gently smoothing his hair.

"He's beautiful," I said. Miguel Antonio had jet-black hair and light brown skin.

Dr. De Catalogne walked in, looking frazzled. "I am sorry," he said. "I was caught in traffic, but I see that everything is fine."

"He was in hurry to be born," Dr. Casanova said, laughing.

Laura appeared fatigued but happy. "How are you feeling?" I asked, holding her hand.

"I have chills, but other than that I am fine," she said, shivering.

Then she added, "Actually, I am hungry; I'd love a big, juicy hamburger." We both laughed.

As I left the hospital on my way home to tell Wanda and my family the good news, I remembered my father's wise, unforgettable words in a letter he had sent me when Pancholín was born: *Recuerda lo que te decía—que los hijos se quieren al par del ama y no hay cosa igual en este mundo como ellos.* Remember what I used to tell you—that we love our children like our own soul and there is nothing like them in the world.

Taking Hold

The completion of my doctorate and promotion to assistant professor fueled even more my desire to use my education to help create a more just and inclusive society. I would continue to advance the study of Mexican and Mexican American literature and culture in the United States through my teaching and research; and by my writing I would go on with my efforts to chronicle the migrant experience, an important and integral part of the American experience. Miguelito's birth also increased my aspiration to provide my growing family with a secure and stable life—different from the one I had as a child. Laura and I yearned to return to California and raise Pancholín and Miguelito near our families, away from the tough, noisy city.

The possibility of our dream becoming a reality came when I received a call from Father John Gray, professor of English and dean of the College of Humanities at the University of Santa Clara. I had met him when I was an undergraduate at Santa Clara, and Laura had taken classes from him during her senior year. He wished to know how we were doing and how far along I was in my graduate studies. I told him about our growing family and that I had just finished the doctorate and was recently promoted to assistant professor. Sounding pleased, he informed me that there might be a faculty position open in the Department of Modern Languages and Literatures beginning that fall. "Are you interested?" he asked.

"I am . . . very much so."

"I can't promise you anything," Father Gray said. "But send me your resumé and a letter indicating your interest and availability."

I immediately requested that Columbia's Office of University Placement and Career Services send Father Gray my dossier, which contained my graduate school transcript and letters of recommendation. I also sent him an application letter. Laura and I kept our fingers crossed and prayed for the job to come through.

And it did. On April 29 I received a letter from Professor Victor Vari, chairman of the Department of Modern Languages and Literatures, offering me a position as an assistant professor. *I apologize for the late notice. The wheels of administration turn very slowly*, he wrote. Professor Vari had been my professor and mentor at Santa Clara.

Laura and I were thrilled. Our dream was no longer just a dream. We were moving back to California to be closer to our families. And returning to my alma mater was ideal for me because I sought to teach at an institution that not only valued teaching and research but also stressed the intellectual moral, spiritual, and social development of students. At Columbia the emphasis was on research and publication and the development of students' minds.

I accepted the offer from Santa Clara and notified Columbia that I would be leaving after fulfilling my commitment to teach during the first session of summer school, which ended the last week in June.

On May 16, the day after Columbia University's commencement, Professor Iduarte and Graciela came over to say goodbye. They were going to spend the summer in their home in Mexico City. *"Allá tienen su casa,"* he said, inviting us to visit them in Mexico. He wrote down the address on his business card and handed it to me.

"I hope you'll visit us in California," I said. "Our home is your home as well. Once we know our new address, we'll send it to you."

"I am retiring in two years," Professor Iduarte said. "We'll make it a point to visit you then."

"We love the Bay Area," Graciela said. "We visited San Francisco many years ago. It's one of the most beautiful and romantic cities we've seen."

I took pictures of Professor Iduarte and Graciela sitting on the sofa, with Pancholín sitting on the professor's lap and Laura holding Miguelito in her arms.

A few days later Professor Susana Redondo de Feldman

also came over to say farewell. She, too, was going away on vacation with her husband. As a parting gift, she gave us a Lladró figurine of Sancho Panza. *"El juego es complete."* The set is complete, she said. We thanked her and promised to keep in touch.

Unfortunately, the University of Santa Clara did not provide faculty with housing, and our lease on the De Morelos's apartment ended on the last day in June, with a two-day grace period. Laura and I decided that she and Pancholín and Miguelito would fly back to California two weeks ahead of me. They would stay with Laura's parents, who offered to help her find a place for us to rent as close to the university as possible. I would join them once summer school was over. It was a painful decision because we would be apart again, but it was a wise choice, as we would avoid repeating the agonizing experience we had when we first moved to New York City and had no definite place to live.

Laura and I packed our belongings, including my books, in the old army trunk and cardboard boxes and shipped them to Laura's parents' home in San Carlos.

On Sunday morning, June 17, I accompanied Laura and our two sons to Kennedy Airport. It was a busy morning as passengers scurried in all directions. I carried Pancholín on my left arm and our suitcase in my right hand. Laura held Miguelito in her arms. Once we checked the luggage and got boarding passes, we went up the elevator to Terminal 7. Pancholín kept tapping on the side of my face and pointing to things along the way and asking, "Wat's that? Wat's that?" When we got to the gate, Laura sat down and I held Pancholín's hand while he pressed his nose against the window and stared in awe at the airplanes taking off like large birds. As I watched him, a flash of memory crossed my mind: I was twelve years old and picking strawberries alongside Roberto and my father in Santa Maria. We would crouch down as crop-dusters flew above our heads and sprayed the fields with chemicals that caused our eyes to burn and water for days.

As the loud announcement was made that the flight was ready to board, I felt my throat tighten. I tugged at Pancholín to follow me to where Laura and the baby were sitting. Laura's eyes welled up as she stood and faced me. She handed me Miguelito, adjusted Pancholín's jacket, and got in line, holding his hand. When the flight attendant took their boarding passes, I handed Miguelito back to her, kissed all three, and said goodbye. As they walked down the ramp, I could hear Pancholín crying, "Daddy, I want Daddy." I wiped my eyes with the back of my hand, moved to the window, and pressed my forehead against it as I watched the plane taxi out of the terminal and onto the runway. Just short of the runway, it stopped. I waved my arms, hoping they could see me. The plane started to move again, this time with increasing speed, until it ascended miles in the air and disappeared into billowing clouds.

On my way back to Manhattan on the subway, I felt a deep ache in my heart and a crushing, suffocating pain in my chest. When I entered the De Morelos apartment, an intense feeling of loneliness enveloped me. I had experienced loneliness many times before: when my parents left me alone all day in the *carcachita*, our old jalopy, to take care of my infant brother while they and Roberto went off into the fields to pick cotton; when, after being deported to Mexico and coming back legally, Roberto and I lived alone in Bonetti Ranch while our parents and younger siblings remained in Mexico and joined us months later (I was fourteen at the time); when I left home to attend college; and, again, during the first two years of graduate school at Columbia. But the loneliness I felt now was far deeper, more painful.

Every day after teaching class I went home to an empty, silent apartment, feeling a knot and burning sensation in my stomach.

What sustained me during those difficult days were Laura's phone calls, my teaching, and the Virgen de Guadalupe, to whom I prayed every night for my family and for time to pass swiftly.

Two days after summer school ended, I bought a one-way airline ticket to San Francisco. I packed my small brown suitcase, locked the door behind me, turned in the apartment key to the building superintendent, and headed to the airport.

During the long flight I thought about how, as a child, I had longed for stability in my life and a place to call my own. This yearning, in large part, came out of a desire to attend school without interruption, without moving from place to place and following seasonal crops. I had now completed my formal education and was finally settling in Santa Clara with my own family.

My heart began racing the moment the plane landed. I un-buckled the seat belt, retrieved my suitcase from the bin, and impatiently waited for people ahead of me to move quickly. As I exited the plane, I saw Pancholín running toward me with outstretched arms, crying, "Daddy, Daddy!" Laura fol-lowed him, holding Miguelito in her arms and smiling from ear to ear. I rushed to Pancholín, scooped him up, and kissed him and hugged him tightly. Holding him in my left arm, I hurried to meet Laura and Miguelito. Hugging them with my right arm, I gave them quick and gentle kisses. "Welcome home," Laura said. She looked tired but happy.

I carried both boys, one in each arm, with Laura by my side, and headed home to Santa Clara, where Laura had rented one side of a two-bedroom duplex at 2018 Harrison Street, half a mile from my alma mater, where I hoped to teach for many years to come.

A Note from the Author

*T*aking Hold, like my previous works, *The Circuit: Stories
from the Life of a Migrant Child*, *Breaking Through*, and
Reaching Out, is autobiographical. In this book I relate the
memorable and life-changing experiences I had living in New
York City while attending Columbia University—the intellectual, emotional, and psychological impact that graduate
studies had on my sense of self; the challenges I faced in completing my formal education; and my efforts to find stability
and purpose in my personal and professional life.

I have described events in chronological order from the
perspective of the young adult I was then, making use of my
powers of imagination and invention to approximate or create dialogue and to fill in small details I have forgotten with
the passage of time.

The genesis of *Taking Hold* and my other works goes

back to the time I was in college, where I quickly discovered that my experiences growing up in a family of migrant
workers were both an obstacle and a blessing. I did not have
the social, economic, and educational advantages that most
of my classmates enjoyed, yet these experiences served as a
constant reminder of how fortunate I was to be in college.
Whenever I felt discouraged, I would write down childhood
memories to give me the courage not to give up. I compare
my situation then to a man who is drowning. A man who
is drowning uses water, the very substance that threatens
his life, to save himself, so I used those experiences that
initially pulled me down to boost myself up. Those recollections served me well my first two years in graduate school.
At times when I felt dispirited, I turned to them to give me
courage and strength.

Following the advice of Professor Iduarte to write and
publish my stories, I gathered my notes and wrote "*La mudanza*," The Move, which I expanded and titled "*Cajas de
carton*," Cardboard Boxes. I translated it into English under
the title "The Circuit" and it was published in the *Arizona
Quarterly* in 1973. After that year, I spent most of my time
teaching and doing scholarly research and administrative
work. It was not until my sabbatical in 1995 that I resumed
writing to chronicle part of my family's history and, more
important, to voice the experiences of a large sector of our
society that has been frequently ignored. Through my writ-

ing I hope to give readers an insight into the lives of Mexican immigrants, some of whom are migrant farm workers, whose courage, struggles, and hopes and dreams for a better life for their children and their children's children give meaning to the term "the American dream." Their story is the American story.

ABOVE: Estefania Jiménez Hernández, Francisco's paternal grandmother.

ABOVE: Luciano and Martiana Moreno Hernández, Francisco's maternal great-grandparents.

RIGHT: Francisco, Roberto, and Trampita in Tent City, Santa Maria, California.

ABOVE LEFT: Roberto and Francisco with their mother.

ABOVE: Francisco, age eight, in Corcoran, California.

BELOW: Francisco's father, Trampita, and Don Pancho, a family friend, at Bonetti Ranch.

ABOVE: Trampita and Francisco in plum orchard, Santa Clara, California.

ABOVE: Francisco, second year of graduate school at Columbia University.

ABOVE: Francisco, age thirteen, at Bonetti Ranch, Santa Maria, California.

LEFT: Francisco's mother and his younger brother Ruben, picking strawberries, Santa Maria, California.

ABOVE: Professor Andrés Iduarte, Francisco's thesis advisor, and Graciela, his wife.

RIGHT: Professor Susana Redondo de Feldman, Francisco's teacher and colleague at Columbia.

BELOW: Photo of Columbia riots.

LEFT: Francisco and Laura's wedding.

ABOVE: Francisco in Grymes Hill apartment.

BELOW: Francisco teaching at Notre Dame Academy High School, Staten Island.

ABOVE: Laura and Pancholín,
Columbia University campus.

ABOVE: Francisco and Pancholín.

BELOW: Francisco and Pancholín on top of the Sundial, Columbia University.

ABOVE: Laura, Pancholín, Francisco, and Miguelito, their second child.

LEFT: Left to right: Professor Iduarte, Pancholín, Laura, Miguelito, and Francisco.

Francisco in his office, Santa Clara University.